DRAMA CLASSICS

The Drama Classics series aims to offer the world's greatest plays in affordable paperback editions for students, actors and theatregoers. The hallmarks of the series are accessible introductions, uncluttered texts and an overall theatrical perspective.

Given that readers may be encountering a particular play for the first time, the introduction seeks to fill in the theatrical/historical background and to outline the chief themes rather than concentrate on interpretational and textual analysis. Similarly the play-texts themselves are free of footnotes and other interpolations: instead there is an end-glossary of 'difficult' words and phrases.

The texts of the English-language plays in the series have been prepared taking full account of all existing scholarship. The foreign-language plays have been newly translated into a modern English that is both actable and accurate: many of the translators regularly have their work staged professionally.

Edited until his early death by Kenneth McLeish, the Drama Classics series continues with his aim of providing a first-class library of dramatic literature representing the best of world theatre.

Associate editor:
Professor Trevor R. Griffiths
School of Arts and Humanities
University of North London

DRAMA CLASSICS *the first hundred*

The Alchemist
All for Love
Andromache
Antigone
Arden of Faversham
Bacchae
Bartholomew Fair
The Beaux Stratagem
The Beggar's Opera
Birds
The Broken Jug
The Changeling
The Cherry Orchard
Children of the Sun
El Cid
The Country Wife
Cyrano de Bergerac
The Dance of Death
The Devil is an
    Ass
Doctor Faustus
A Doll's House
Don Juan
The Duchess of
    Malfi
Edward II
Electra (Euripides)
Electra (Sophocles)
An Enemy of the
    People
The Eunuch
Every Man in his
    Humour
Everyman
The Father
Faust
A Flea in her Ear
Frogs
Fuenteovejuna
The Game of Love
    and Chance

Ghosts
The Government
    Inspector
Hedda Gabler
The Hypochondriac
The Importance of
    Being Earnest
An Ideal Husband
An Italian Straw Hat
The Jew of Malta
The Lady from the Sea
The Learned Ladies
Life is a Dream
The Lower Depths
The Lucky Chance
Lulu
Lysistrata
The Magistrate
The Malcontent
The Man of Mode
The Marriage of
    Figaro
Mary Stuart
The Master Builder
Medea
Menaechmi
The Misanthrope
The Miser
Miss Julie
A Month in the
    Country
A New Way to Pay
    Old Debts
Oedipus at Kolonos
Oedipus the King
The Oresteia
Peer Gynt
Phaedra
Philoctetes
The Playboy of the
    Western World

The Recruiting
    Officer
The Revenger's
    Tragedy
The Rivals
The Robbers
La Ronde
Rosmersholm
The Rover
The School for
    Scandal
The Seagull
The Servant of Two
    Masters
She Stoops to
    Conquer
The Shoemaker's
    Holiday
The Spanish Tragedy
Spring's Awakening
Tartuffe
Thérèse Raquin
Three Sisters
'Tis Pity She's a
    Whore
Too Clever by Half
Ubu
Uncle Vanya
Vassa Zheleznova
Volpone
The Way of the World
The White Devil
The Wild Duck
Women Beware
    Women
Women of Troy
Woyzeck

*The publishers welcome
suggestions for further titles*

DRAMA CLASSICS

SHE STOOPS TO CONQUER

by

Oliver Goldsmith

edited and with an introduction by
Trevor R. Griffiths

NICK HERN BOOKS

London

A Drama Classic

This edition of *She Stoops to Conquer* first published in Great Britain as a paperback original in 1999 by Nick Hern Books Limited, 14 Larden Road, London W3 7ST

Copyright in the introduction © 1999 Nick Hern Books

Copyright in this edition of the text © 1999 Trevor R. Griffiths

Typeset by Country Setting, Kingsdown, Kent CT14 8ES
Printed by Bath Press, Avon

A CIP catalogue record for this book is available from the British Library

ISBN 1 85459 441 9

Introduction

Oliver Goldsmith

Goldsmith was born in Pallas, County Longford, Ireland, in 1728 or 1730, the son of a church minister. He studied, without great success, at Trinity College, Dublin, and the universities of Edinburgh, Leyden and Padua. Although he studied medicine, acquiring the title Doctor along the way, his claim to it appears to have been dubious. Addicted to gambling, at which he was never very successful, he scraped a living as an assistant to an apothecary and as an assistant teacher in a school before drifting into journalism. He established his reputation with his 'Chinese letters' (1760), in which he adopted the persona of a Chinese tourist to satirise contemporary manners. This work led to his friendship with Samuel Johnson (1709-1784) and a respected place in London literary life. His first play *The Good-Natured Man* (1768) was not a great success. *She Stoops to Conquer*, his second play, was eventually produced to critical acclaim in 1773 despite the initial reservations of the London theatre managers. Goldsmith's death in 1774 may have been partly caused by his own misdiagnosis of his condition. He appears to have been a likeable but disorganised character, constantly short of money, who once failed to emigrate to America because he missed the boat. The central mistake of *She Stoops to Conquer* was, he claimed, based on one of his own errors when he mistook a gentleman's house for an inn. Apart from *She Stoops*, he is now best remembered for his novel, *The Vicar of Wakefield* (1766), an ironic recasting of the biblical story of Job, and his poem, *The Deserted Village* (1770), an attack on the enclosure of common land.

She Stoops to Conquer: **What Happens in the Play**

1.1 Mr and Mrs Hardcastle live in an old house with their daughter Kate, Tony Lumpkin (Mrs Hardcastle's son by her first marriage) and Constance Neville (her niece). Mrs Hardcastle controls Constance's fortune and hopes to marry her to Tony, who cannot legally refuse her because he is not yet of age. At the beginning of the play they are expecting young Marlow, son of Sir Charles Marlow, Hardcastle's friend, as a suitor for Kate. Hardcastle insists that Kate always dresses plainly in the evening, a demand that will have a significant effect on the plot.

1.2 Marlow and his friend Hastings, who is Constance's admirer, have lost their way and arrive at an alehouse where Tony and his friends are drinking. Tony directs them to the Hardcastles' house but tells them that it is an inn.

2 Hardcastle drills his servants in appropriate manners. The two young men arrive, treating him disdainfully, as an innkeeper rather than a gentleman. Constance meets Hastings and explains the mistake but they decide not to tell Marlow in case he leaves out of embarrassment. Marlow has a formal meeting with Kate, believing she too has arrived at the supposed inn, and Hastings enlists Tony to help him to elope with Constance.

3 Hardcastle and Kate compare notes about Marlow and find that they disagree wildly about him. Tony has obtained Constance's jewels (her fortune) from Mrs Hardcastle and gives them to Hastings. Mrs Hardcastle discovers that they are missing. Kate discovers that Marlow had not actually looked at her during their meeting but had later admired her in her plain dress, believing her to be the barmaid. When she meets Marlow again (still in her plain dress), he behaves very differently, attempting to seduce her. Hardcastle discovers them and allows Kate an hour to convince him that Marlow is a suitable suitor.

4 Marlow has had the jewels returned to Mrs Hardcastle, whom he still believes to be the landlady, and continues to get into deeper water with Mr Hardcastle. As they quarrel the truth begins to emerge. Marlow discovers more of the truth from Kate, although she still doesn't reveal her true identity. Tony and Constance pretend to flirt while waiting for the horses to be ready for Hastings and Constance to elope. Unfortunately Hastings has sent Tony a note which, being virtually illiterate, he cannot read; Mrs Hardcastle reads the note, discovers the proposed elopement and commandeers the horses and carriage to take Constance away to her aunt's.

5 Sir Charles has arrived and Marlow is mortified. He and Kate separately give their fathers contradictory accounts of their relationship. Tony reappears in the garden having taken his mother and Constance on a long circular journey back to where they started from. Mrs Hardcastle mistakes Hardcastle for a highwayman and Constance decides that she cannot face another attempt to elope. Hidden, Sir Charles and Hardcastle observe Marlow meet Kate, whom he still thinks is a barmaid. Amazed at what he hears, Sir Charles intervenes and Marlow discovers who Kate really is. Convinced by Constance and Hastings's repentance, Hardcastle reveals that Tony is actually legally old enough to refuse to marry Constance, at which point she gets control of her fortune and can therefore marry Hastings. The play ends with Hardcastle joining Kate and Marlow's hands.

dedication to Dr Johnson, of Colman's reluctance and of the danger of 'undertaking a comedy, not merely sentimental'.

She Stoops attacks sentimentalism in several ways. Goldsmith satirises the Sentimental directly in scenes such as Marlow's wooing of Kate where hypocrisy is foregrounded and the cult of sentimentality is exposed as a sham. He also includes characters (particularly Tony) and scenes that a sentimentalist would regard as vulgar, such as the drinking scene in the Three Pigeons where low life characters behave in an uncouth fashion (although he also attacks sentimentalism here with the dancing bear that only dances to genteel tunes). When he does use scenes and characters that draw on the sentimental tradition, he embeds them in a matrix of contrasting perspectives. For example, the most straightforwardly sentimental characters in the play are Constance and Hastings: you can hear it in the way they talk and in the kinds of attitudes they strike. But Constance and Hastings (rather stiff and stereotypical in their dialogue, their attitudes, and their actions) are at one end of a spectrum, with Tony (savage and uneducated, given to straight talking and his own pleasure, the stereotyped English country squire familiar from eighteenth century novels like Fielding's *Tom Jones*, 1749) at the other. In the middle are Kate and Marlow, two characters who are able ultimately to transcend stereotypes by uniting two contradictory sets of characteristics to create whole people.

The play's ending is an attack on the sentimental mode (Mrs Hardcastle herself compares it to the whining end of a modern novel), but the discoveries in the last act untie the knots that the plot has got us into and enable the protagonists to marry whom they want to. Comedies often resolve their plot complications by a discovery that the lower class beloved is actually a princess in disguise or that a legal prohibition is actually unenforceable. In *She Stoops*, the supposed social barrier to marriage disappears when the barmaid turns out to be the heiress, a part parody of some of the features of the traditional ending that still maintains some of its emotional appeal. The second discovery, that Tony is of age, would, traditionally, allow him to marry despite parental opposition but here, ironically, it permits him to refuse to marry Constance, thus clearing the way for her marriage to Hastings. Romantic comedies usually involve possible twists and turns between at least two young people of each gender but there is actually no romantic pain in this play since Hastings' initial jealousy of Tony is clearly ridiculous and we know from early on that Marlow's difficulties with his two love objects are apparent rather than real.

However, not everyone is reconciled: Mrs Hardcastle may have had the stuffing knocked out of her by the cross country journey and may have been an object of ridicule when she mistook her husband for a highway-man, but at the end she shows no sign of joining in the comic resolution. Similarly Goldsmith's comic universe recognises that no amount of his mother making him waistcoats will make Tony Lumpkin genteel. A far from Noble Savage, Tony, easily the lowest character in the play, is left free to squander his fortune on horses, dogs, drink and Bett Bouncer.

Comedy of Manners and Dramatic Irony

English comedies from the Restoration period and similar works, such as *She Stoops*, in which the social conventions and customs of a leisured class sustain the dramatic impetus are often described as Comedies of Manners. They are often defined in terms which suggest a superficial concern with fashions, decorum and etiquette, but their starting point is the view that human behaviour is patterned and consists of systems of codes and conventions (often implicit rather than explicit) which impose an order on experience by making it predictable and manageable. Comedies of Manners may test the limits of social codes and reveal their arbitrariness, but they normally end with a restoration of order through, as in *She Stoops*, multiple betrothals or marriages that channel potentially anarchic energies into socially acceptable forms.

Comedies of Manners can scrutinise the values enshrined in a social code, comparing and contrasting them with those that people actually live by. In *She Stoops* the various mistakes about locations lead the characters, particularly Marlow, to adopt behaviour which is clearly inappropriate to its actual context rather than its supposed one. The new context in turn reveals that such behaviour is inappropriate for any context because it treats people as stereotypes rather than individuals. In particular, Marlow's treatment of women reveals the central inadequacy of the socially prescribed ways of dealing with women. *She Stoops* also uses its farcical and romantic elements to explore the realities underlying various deceptions, using dramatic irony, the pleasure that the audience feels in being more aware of the facts than the characters are, as a way of exploring the discrepancies between reality and appearance. Only when the various mistaken identities and locations are revealed can the split personalities be healed and a new synthesis emerge to replace the old failed system.

The dramatist who writes Comedy of Manners must always try to discover ways of guiding the audience's reactions to the portrayal of manners if the audience is not simply to accept the reflection of those manners as uncritical praise of them. The laughter should be uncomfortable and questioning rather than comforting and affirmative. Because of that interrogative element, good Comedies of Manners like *She Stoops to Conquer* survive when the actual manners depicted and mocked have long since vanished. The basic questions the play asks remain important: how should people behave towards each other, how can society's patterns adequately reflect people's real needs and aspirations?

Education, Town and Country

The play's overall impact is heightened by the ways in which the skirmishes between Kate and Marlow are surrounded by groups of characters placed at different points on a spectrum to reinforce Goldsmith's development of the plot and to offer systematic structural contrasts and comparisons with their developing relationship, using education, sentiment and the country as touchstones in this process. Tony, Marlow and Hastings, for example, represent three possible ways in which a young man might behave: Tony is a wild roaring prankster out of parental control and ruined by his education or lack of it; Hastings is a sentimental and conventional lover; Marlow, also ruined by his education, oscillates wildly between the two extremes. Tony is almost a force of nature, who corrects the behaviour of the town by setting up his pranks and intervenes to help the lovers. Like his half-sister Kate, he has a practical way of dealing with issues that contrasts sharply with the more townified manners of Constance, Hastings and Marlow. The untutored rustic simplicity of the servants corrects Hardcastle's rhetorical preferences for old things and the ways of the country, while the absurdly metropolitan pretensions of Mrs Hardcastle offer a further angle on the town/country divide.

Goldsmith's dramatic method reinforces the play's central preoccupation with the importance and necessity of discovering true natures and true identities. Though Tony's coming of age also has a crucial bearing on that process, the relationship between Kate and Marlow is central, with each of them playing a number of roles as they perform their courtship dance. The dance does not, of course, take them into a fully developed mature relationship but it does clear the ground for one as well as giving them shared experience on which to build.

Courtship, Engagement, Marriage

The obstacles to a marriage of true minds in *She Stoops* stem from the workings of a society that prescribes a way of proceeding for male/female relationships that virtually prevents them from succeeding. The idea of marriage as a romantic union entered into by two individuals based on mutual love may still predominate in Western society, but it is by no means universal historically, geographically or socially. Arranged marriages would have been the norm in the Hardcastles' class in this society at this period. One of the duties of a father was to make sure that his daughter was married appropriately, that is to someone who would provide a secure economic basis for them and their children. An enlightened father (such as Hardcastle) allowed his daughters a right of veto over suitably vetted candidates.

Unfortunately for Constance and Hastings, the death of her father has allowed Mrs Hardcastle to assume the role of guardian and to cut off Hastings's legitimate courtship of Constance in favour of her mercenary aspirations for Tony. Marlow is clearly financially eligible to be Kate's husband but, having been educated in single sex schools and colleges, and choosing to spend his leisure time in inns, he is a prime example of the double standard of sexual morality: he has no way of dealing with women except as goddesses or as whores. However, throughout the play he is presented as being aware of and unhappy with this aspect of his personality. There is of course an underlying irony in the presentation of the various courtships that both marriage (which is seen as the proper male-female relationship) and prostitution (which is seen as improper) are presented as relying heavily on an economic bargain.

Marlow clearly operates by different sets of values, not only when dealing with Kate in her two dresses but also in his general dealings with those who appear to be of a lower social station than himself. Kate, however, consciously adopts roles in order to perform the necessary therapy which will make Marlow into a whole man. Marlow wants to unite the two sides of his personality so that he can treat women as people. At the end of the play, confronted with the inescapable fact that both the barmaid and the sober sentimental lady are the same woman, he is forced to realise that it is possible to adopt a different and more wholesome approach in which two attitudes are not in conflict. So the ending of the play is not simply one in which the mistakes of a night are corrected, it is one in which the leading characters have undergone significant change in the course of the night and in which a new and better order has emerged from the old.

Deception and Disguise

She Stoops to Conquer begins with deception and disguise: no-one is what they seem: Old Hardcastle is not an inn-keeper, Kate is not a bar-maid or a poor relation, the house is not an inn, the garden is not Crackskull Common, Marlow is both a rake and a genteel gentleman and so on. As an audience we are aware throughout the play of the most significant deceptions so part of our pleasure arises simply from knowing more than the characters and thus being able to anticipate the outcomes of their difficulties. Only Tony's date of birth is actually hidden from us so that on every other major issue we are able to anticipate the plot's resolution. The process of discovery and enlightenment brings together at the end what seemed like irreconcilable polarities at the beginning. Marlow and Kate are the main beneficiaries of this process because they are moved from unhappiness to a shared recognition of their true natures which provides the basis for a mutual understanding and, since this is comedy, the basis of a happy marriage.

The continuing success of the play may stem in part from our pleasure as an audience in our ability to read the social and theatrical codes more effectively than the characters; perhaps we also derive pleasure from watching characters discover a 'real' identity that enables them to make sense of their lives and which, in turn, helps us to fantasise a wholeness in our own lives. It is the play's comic exploration of these important questions of identity and self discovery that makes a major contribution to its success. It may start as a comedy of errors, of deceptions and intrigues, but it becomes a comedy of discovery and enlightenment.

Trevor R Griffiths

This edition is based on the first edition of 1773, with lightly modernised spelling, punctuation and stage directions. The section on Georgian theatre is by Colin Counsell.

For Further Reading

John Ginger's *The Notable Man: the Life and Times of Oliver Goldsmith* (Hamilton, 1977) is a useful biography, complemented by E. H. Mikhail's collection of contemporary biographical material in *Goldsmith: Interviews and Recollections* (Macmillan 1993). J. B. Lyons discusses *The Mystery of Oliver Goldsmith's Medical Degree* (Carraig Books, 1978) and G. S. Rousseau has traced the history of responses to Goldsmith's work in *Oliver Goldsmith: the Critical Heritage* (Routledge, 1974).

Richard W. Bevis's *English Drama: Restoration and Eighteenth Century, 1660-1789* (Longman, 1988) is a perceptive and comprehensive modern look at the period as a whole which provides a useful context for Goldsmith's work. Katharine J. Worth's *Sheridan and Goldsmith* (Macmillan, 1992) and John Loftis's *Sheridan and the Drama of Georgian England* (Blackwell, 1976) are useful on Goldsmith. D. J. Palmer's Casebook *Comedy: Developments in Criticism* (Macmillan, 1984) reprints key extracts from the debate on comedy that Goldsmith was involved in.

Goldsmith: Key Dates

1728	*c*, or 1730. Born in Pallas, County Longford, Ireland.
1745-9	Student at Trinity College, Dublin.
1752-3	Medical student at Edinburgh.
1753-6	Travelled and studied in Europe.
1756	Settled in London.
1759	*An Enquiry into the Present State of Polite Learning in Europe* published.
1760	Published 'Chinese Letters' in periodical *The Bee*.
1762	'Chinese Letters' published in book form as *The Citizen of the World*.
1764	*An History of England in a Series of Letters...* published. *The Traveller* (poem) published.
1766	*The Vicar of Wakefield* (novel) published.
1767	*Poems for Young Ladies* published.
1768	*The Good Natured Man* performed and published.
1769	*The Roman History* published.
1770	*The Deserted Village* (poem) published; Professor of Ancient History at the Royal Academy.
1771	*The History of England* published.
1773	*She Stoops to Conquer*, performed and published.
1774	Dies, 4 April. *Retaliation* (poem) *The Grecian History* and *An History of the Earth and Animated Nature* published posthumously.

SHE STOOPS TO CONQUER

To Samuel Johnson, L.L.D.

Dear Sir,

By inscribing this slight performance to you, I do not mean so much to compliment you as myself. It may do me some honour to inform the public, that I have lived many years in intimacy with you. It may serve the interests of mankind also to inform them, that the greatest wit may be found in a character, without impairing the most unaffected piety.

I have, particularly, reason to thank you for your partiality to this performance. The undertaking a comedy, not merely sentimental, was very dangerous; and Mr Colman, who saw this piece in its various stages, always thought it so. However I ventured to trust it to the public; and though it was necessarily delayed till late in the season, I have every reason to be grateful.

I am, Dear Sir,
Your most sincere friend,
And admirer,

OLIVER GOLDSMITH

Prologue

by David Garrick, Esq.

Enter MR WOODWARD,
dressed in black, and holding a handkerchief to his eyes.

Excuse me, sirs, I pray – I can't yet speak –
I'm crying now – and have been all the week!
'Tis not alone this mourning suit, good masters;
I've that within – for which there are no plasters!
Pray would you know the reason why I'm crying?
The Comic muse, long sick, is now a-dying!
And if she goes, my tears will never stop;
For as a player, I can't squeeze out one drop:
I am undone, that's all – shall lose my bread –
I'd rather, but that's nothing – lose my head.
When the sweet maid is laid upon the bier,
Shuter and I shall be chief mourners here.
To her a mawkish drab of spurious breed,
Who deals in sentimentals, will succeed!
Poor Ned and I are dead to all intents,
We can as soon speak Greek as sentiments!
Both nervous grown, to keep our spirits up,
We now and then take down a hearty cup.
What shall we do? – If Comedy forsake us!
They'll turn us out, and no one else will take us;
But why can't I be moral? – Let me try –
My heart thus pressing – fixed my face and eye –
With a sententious look, that nothing means,

(Faces are blocks, in sentimental scenes)
Thus I begin – 'All is not gold that glitters,
Pleasure seems sweet, but proves a glass of bitters.
When ignorance enters, folly is at hand;
Learning is better far than house and land:
Let not your virtue trip, who trips may stumble,
And virtue is not virtue, if she tumble.'

I give it up – morals won't do for me;
To make you laugh I must play tragedy.
One hope remains – hearing the maid was ill,
A doctor comes this night to show his skill.
To cheer her heart, and give your muscles motion,
He in five draughts prepared, presents a potion:
A kind of magic charm – for be assured,
If you will swallow it, the maid is cured:
But desperate the Doctor, and her case is,
If you reject the dose, and make wry faces!
This truth he boasts, will boast it while he lives,
No poisonous drugs are mixed in what he gives;
Should he succeed, you'll give him his degree;
If not, within he will receive no fee!
The college *you*, must his pretensions back,
Pronounce him regular, or dub him quack.

6

Dramatis Personae

Men

SIR CHARLES MARLOW

YOUNG [CHARLES] MARLOW, *his son*

HARDCASTLE

[GEORGE] HASTINGS

TONY LUMPKIN

DIGGORY

Women

MRS HARDCASTLE

MISS [KATE] HARDCASTLE

MISS [CONSTANCE] NEVILLE

MAID

LANDLORD, SERVANTS, *etc. etc.*

Act I, Scene i

Scene. A chamber in an old fashioned house.

Enter MRS HARDCASTLE *and* MR HARDCASTLE.

MRS HARDCASTLE. I vow, Mr Hardcastle, you're very particular. Is there a creature in the whole country, but ourselves, that does not take a trip to town now and then, to rub off the rust a little? There's the two Miss Hoggs, and our neighbour, Mrs Grigsby, go to take a month's polishing every winter.

HARDCASTLE. Ay, and bring back vanity and affectation to last them the whole year. I wonder why London cannot keep its own fools at home? In my time, the follies of the town crept slowly among us, but now they travel faster than a stagecoach. Its fopperies come down, not only as inside passengers, but in the very basket.

MRS HARDCASTLE. Ay, *your* times were fine times, indeed; you have been telling us of *them* for many a long year. Here we live in an old rumbling mansion, that looks for all the world like an inn, but that we never see company. Our best visitors are old Mrs Oddfish, the curate's wife, and little Cripplegate, the lame dancing-master: and all our entertainment your old stories of Prince Eugene and the Duke of Marlborough. I hate such old-fashioned trumpery.

HARDCASTLE. And I love it. I love everything that's old: old friends, old times, old manners, old books, old wine; and I believe, Dorothy, (*Taking her hand.*) you'll own I have been pretty fond of an old wife.

MRS HARDCASTLE. Lord, Mr Hardcastle, you're for ever at your 'Dorothys' and your 'old wifes'. You may be a Darby, but I'll be no Joan, I promise you. I'm not so old as you'd make me, by more than one good year. Add twenty to twenty, and make money of that.

HARDCASTLE. Let me see; twenty added to twenty, makes just fifty and seven.

MRS HARDCASTLE. It's false, Mr Hardcastle: I was but twenty when I was brought to bed of Tony, that I had by Mr Lumpkin, my first husband; and he's not come to years of discretion yet.

HARDCASTLE. Nor ever will, I dare answer for him. Ay, you have taught *him* finely.

MRS HARDCASTLE. No matter, Tony Lumpkin has a good fortune. My son is not to live by his learning. I don't think a boy wants much learning to spend fifteen hundred a year.

HARDCASTLE. Learning, quotha! A mere composition of tricks and mischief.

MRS HARDCASTLE. Humour, my dear: nothing but humour. Come, Mr Hardcastle, you must allow the boy a little humour.

HARDCASTLE. I'd sooner allow him an horse-pond. If burning the footmen's shoes, frighting the maids, and worrying the kittens, be humour, he has it. It was but yesterday he fastened my wig to the back of my chair, and when I went to make a bow, I popped my bald head in Mrs Frizzle's face.

MRS HARDCASTLE. And am I to blame? The poor boy was always too sickly to do any good. A school would be his death. When he comes to be a little stronger, who knows what a year or two's Latin may do for him?

HARDCASTLE. Latin for him! A cat and fiddle. No, no, the ale-house and the stable are the only schools he'll ever go to.

MRS HARDCASTLE. Well, we must not snub the poor boy now, for I believe we shan't have him long among us. Anybody that looks in his face may see he's consumptive.

HARDCASTLE. Ay, if growing too fat be one of the symptoms.

MRS HARDCASTLE. He coughs sometimes.

HARDCASTLE. Yes, when his liquor goes the wrong way.

MRS HARDCASTLE. I'm actually afraid of his lungs.

HARDCASTLE. And truly so am I; for he sometimes whoops like a speaking trumpet –

TONY *hallooing behind the scenes.*

– Oh there he goes – A very consumptive figure, truly.

Enter TONY, *crossing the stage.*

MRS HARDCASTLE. Tony, where are you going, my charmer? Won't you give papa and I a little of your company, lovey?

TONY. I'm in haste, mother, I cannot stay.

MRS HARDCASTLE. You shan't venture out this raw evening, my dear: you look most shockingly.

TONY. I can't stay, I tell you. The Three Pigeons expects me down every moment. There's some fun going forward.

HARDCASTLE. Ay; the ale-house, the old place: I thought so.

MRS HARDCASTLE. A low, paltry set of fellows.

TONY. Not so low neither. There's Dick Muggins the exciseman, Jack Slang the horse doctor, Little Aminadab that grinds the music box, and Tom Twist that spins the pewter platter.

MRS HARDCASTLE. Pray, my dear, disappoint them for one night at least.

TONY. As for disappointing *them*, I should not so much mind; but I can't abide to disappoint *myself*.

MRS HARDCASTLE (*detaining him*). You shan't go.

TONY. I will, I tell you.

MRS HARDCASTLE. I say you shan't.

TONY. We'll see which is strongest, you or I.

Exit, hauling her out.

HARDCASTLE. Ay, there goes a pair that only spoil each other. But is not the whole age in a combination to drive sense and discretion out of doors? There's my pretty darling Kate; the fashions of the times have almost infected her too. By living a year or two in town, she is as fond of gauze, and French frippery, as the best of them.

Enter MISS HARDCASTLE.

HARDCASTLE. Blessings on my pretty innocence! Dressed out as usual, my Kate. Goodness! What a quantity of superfluous silk hast thou got about thee, girl! I could never teach the fools of this age, that the indigent world could be clothed out of the trimmings of the vain.

MISS HARDCASTLE. You know our agreement, sir. You allow me the morning to receive and pay visits, and to dress in my own manner; and in the evening, I put on my housewife's dress to please you.

HARDCASTLE. Well, remember I insist on the terms of our agreement; and, by the bye, I believe I shall have occasion to try your obedience this very evening.

MISS HARDCASTLE. I protest, sir, I don't comprehend your meaning.

HARDCASTLE. Then, to be plain with you, Kate, I expect the young gentleman I have chosen to be your husband from town this very day. I have his father's letter, in which he informs me his son is set out, and that he intends to follow himself shortly after.

MISS HARDCASTLE. Indeed! I wish I had known something of this before. Bless me, how shall I behave? It's a thousand to one I shan't like him; our meeting will be so formal, and so like a thing of business, that I shall find no room for friendship or esteem.

HARDCASTLE. Depend upon it, child, I'll never control your choice; but Mr Marlow, whom I have pitched upon, is the son of my old friend, Sir Charles Marlow, of whom you have heard me talk so often. The young gentleman has been bred a scholar, and is designed for an employment in the service of his country. I am told he's a man of an excellent understanding.

MISS HARDCASTLE. Is he?

HARDCASTLE. Very generous.

MISS HARDCASTLE. I believe I shall like him.

HARDCASTLE. Young and brave.

MISS HARDCASTLE. I'm sure I shall like him.

HARDCASTLE. And very handsome.

MISS HARDCASTLE. My dear papa, say no more, (*Kissing his hand.*) he's mine, I'll have him.

HARDCASTLE. And to crown all, Kate, he's one of the most bashful and reserved young fellows in all the world.

MISS HARDCASTLE. Eh! you have frozen me to death again. That word reserved, has undone all the rest of his accomplishments. A reserved lover, it is said, always makes a suspicious husband.

HARDCASTLE. On the contrary, modesty seldom resides in a breast that is not enriched with nobler virtues. It was the very feature in his character that first struck me.

MISS HARDCASTLE. He must have more striking features to catch me, I promise you. However, if he be so young, so handsome, and so everything, as you mention, I believe he'll do still. I think I'll have him.

HARDCASTLE. Ay, Kate, but there is still an obstacle. It's more than an even wager, he may not have *you*.

MISS HARDCASTLE. My dear papa, why will you mortify one so? – Well, if he refuses, instead of breaking my heart at his indifference, I'll break my glass for its flattery, set my cap to some newer fashion, and look out for some less difficult admirer.

HARDCASTLE. Bravely resolved! In the meantime I'll go prepare the servants for his reception; as we seldom see company they want as much training as a company of recruits, the first day's muster.

Exit.

MISS HARDCASTLE. Lud, this news of papa's puts me all in a flutter. Young, handsome; these he put last; but I put them foremost. Sensible, good-natured; I like all that. But then reserved, and sheepish, that's much against him. Yet can't he be cured of his timidity, by being taught to be proud of his wife? Yes, and can't I – But I vow I'm disposing of the husband, before I have secured the lover.

Enter MISS NEVILLE.

MISS HARDCASTLE. I'm glad you're come, Neville, my
dear. Tell me, Constance, how do I look this evening?
Is there anything whimsical about me? Is it one of my well-
looking days, child? Am I in face today?

MISS NEVILLE. Perfectly, my dear. Yet now I look
again – bless me! – sure no accident has happened among
the canary birds or the gold fishes? Has your brother or the
cat been meddling? Or has the last novel been too moving?

MISS HARDCASTLE. No; nothing of all this. I have been
threatened – I can scarce get it out – I have been
threatened with a lover.

MISS NEVILLE. And his name –

MISS HARDCASTLE. Is Marlow.

MISS NEVILLE. Indeed!

MISS HARDCASTLE. The son of Sir Charles Marlow.

MISS NEVILLE. As I live, the most intimate friend of Mr
Hastings, my admirer. They are never asunder. I believe you
must have seen him when we lived in town.

MISS HARDCASTLE. Never.

MISS NEVILLE. He's a very singular character, I assure you.
Among women of reputation and virtue, he is the modestest
man alive; but his acquaintance give him a very different
character among creatures of another stamp: you understand
me.

MISS HARDCASTLE. An odd character, indeed. I shall never
be able to manage him. What shall I do? Pshaw, think no
more of him, but trust to occurrences for success. But how
goes on your own affair my dear, has my mother been
courting you for my brother Tony, as usual?

MISS NEVILLE. I have just come from one of our agreeable tête-à-têtes. She has been saying a hundred tender things, and setting off her pretty monster as the very pink of perfection.

MISS HARDCASTLE. And her partiality is such, that she actually thinks him so. A fortune like yours is no small temptation. Besides, as she has the sole management of it, I'm not surprised to see her unwilling to let it go out of the family.

MISS NEVILLE. A fortune like mine, which chiefly consists in jewels, is no such mighty temptation. But at any rate if my dear Hastings be but constant, I make no doubt to be too hard for her at last. However, I let her suppose that I am in love with her son, and she never once dreams that my affections are fixed upon another.

MISS HARDCASTLE. My good brother holds out stoutly. I could almost love him for hating you so.

MISS NEVILLE. It is a good-natured creature at bottom, and I'm sure would wish to see me married to anybody but himself. But my aunt's bell rings for our afternoon's walk round the improvements. *Allons*. Courage is necessary as our affairs are critical.

MISS HARDCASTLE. Would it were bedtime and all were well.

Exeunt.

Act I, Scene ii

Scene. An Alehouse Room. Several shabby fellows, with punch and tobacco.
TONY *at the head of the table, a little higher than the rest: a mallet in*
his hand.

ALL. Hurrah, hurrah, hurrah, bravo.

FIRST FELLOW Now, gentlemen, silence for a song. The
    Squire is going to knock himself down for a song.

ALL. Ay, a song, a song.

TONY. Then I'll sing you, gentlemen, a song I made upon this
    ale-house, the Three Pigeons.

    Song.

    Let school-masters puzzle their brain,
        With grammar, and nonsense, and learning;
    Good liquor, I stoutly maintain,
        Gives genus a better discerning.
    Let them brag of their Heathenish Gods,
        Their Lethes, their Styxes, and Stygians;
    Their Quis, and their Quæs, and their Quods,
        They're all but a parcel of Pigeons.
        Toroddle, toroddle, toroll.

    When Methodist preachers come down,
        A-preaching that drinking is sinful,
    I'll wager the rascals a crown,
        They always preach best with a skinful.
    But when you come down with your pence,
        For a slice of their scurvy religion,
    I'll leave it to all men of sense,
        But you my good friend are the pigeon.
        Toroddle, toroddle, toroll.

Then come, put the jorum about,
    And let us be merry and clever,
Our hearts and our liquors are stout,
    Here's the Three Jolly Pigeons for ever.
Let some cry up woodcock or hare,
    Your bustards, your ducks, and your widgeons;
But of all the birds in the air,
    Here's a health to the Three Jolly Pigeons.
      Toroddle, toroddle, toroll.

ALL. Bravo, bravo.

FIRST FELLOW. The Squire has got spunk in him.

SECOND FELLOW. I love to hear him sing, bekeays he never
gives us nothing that's low.

THIRD FELLOW. Oh damn anything that's *low*, I cannot bear
it.

FOURTH FELLOW. The genteel thing is the genteel thing at
any time. If so be that a gentleman bees in a concatenation
accordingly.

THIRD FELLOW. I like the maxum of it, Master Muggins.
What though I am obligated to dance a bear, a man may be
a gentleman for all that. May this be my poison if my bear
ever dances but to the very genteelest of tunes. 'Water
parted', or the minuet in *Ariadne*.

SECOND FELLOW. What a pity it is the Squire is not come
to his own. It would be well for all the publicans within ten
miles round of him.

TONY. Ecod and so it would Master Slang. I'd then show
what it was to keep choice of company.

SECOND FELLOW. Oh he takes after his own father for that.
To be sure old Squire Lumpkin was the finest gentleman

I ever set my eyes on. For winding the straight horn, or beating a thicket for a hare, or a wench, he never had his fellow. It was a saying in the place, that he kept the best horses, dogs, and girls in the whole county.

TONY. Ecod, and when I'm of age I'll be no bastard I promise you. I have been thinking of Bet Bouncer and the miller's grey mare to begin with. But come, my boys, drink about and be merry, for you pay no reckoning. Well Stingo, what's the matter?

Enter LANDLORD.

LANDLORD. There be two gentlemen in a post-chaise at the door. They have lost their way upo' the forest; and they are talking something about Mr Hardcastle.

TONY. As sure as can be one of them must be the gentleman that's coming down to court my sister. Do they seem to be Londoners?

LANDLORD. I believe they may. They look woundily like Frenchmen.

TONY. Then desire them to step this way, and I'll set them right in a twinkling.

Exit LANDLORD.

Gentlemen, as they mayn't be good enough company for you, step down for a moment, and I'll be with you in the squeezing of a lemon.

Exeunt MOB.

TONY. Father-in-law has been calling me whelp, and hound, this half-year. Now if I pleased, I could be so revenged upon the old grumbletonian. But then I'm afraid – afraid of what! I shall soon be worth fifteen hundred a year, and let him frighten me out of *that* if he can.

Enter LANDLORD, *conducting* MARLOW *and* HASTINGS.

MARLOW. What a tedious uncomfortable day have we had of it! We were told it was but forty miles across the country, and we have come above threescore.

HASTINGS. And all, Marlow, from that unaccountable reserve of yours, that would not let us enquire more frequently on the way.

MARLOW. I own, Hastings, I am unwilling to lay myself under an obligation to everyone I meet; and often stand the chance of an unmannerly answer.

HASTINGS. At present, however, we are not likely to receive any answer.

TONY. No offence, gentlemen. But I'm told you have been enquiring for one Mr Hardcastle, in these parts. Do you know what part of the country you are in?

HASTINGS. Not in the least, sir, but should thank you for information.

TONY. Nor the way you came?

HASTINGS. No, sir; but if you can inform us –

TONY. Why, gentlemen, if you know neither the road you are going, nor where you are, nor the road you came, the first thing I have to inform you is, that – You have lost your way.

MARLOW. We wanted no ghost to tell us that.

TONY. Pray, gentlemen, may I be so bold as to ask the place from whence you came?

MARLOW. That's not necessary towards directing us where we are to go.

TONY. No offence; but question for question is all fair, you know. Pray, gentlemen, is not this same Hardcastle a cross-grained, old-fashioned, whimsical fellow, with an ugly face, a daughter, and a pretty son?

HASTINGS. We have not seen the gentleman, but he has the family you mention.

TONY. The daughter, a tall trapesing, trolloping, talkative maypole – The son, a pretty, well-bred, agreeable youth, that everybody is fond of.

MARLOW. Our information differs in this. The daughter is said to be well-bred and beautiful; the son, an awkward booby, reared up and spoiled at his mother's apron-string.

TONY. He-he-hem – Then, gentlemen, all I have to tell you is, that you won't reach Mr Hardcastle's house this night, I believe.

HASTINGS. Unfortunate!

TONY. It's a damned long, dark, boggy, dirty, dangerous way. Stingo, tell the gentlemen the way to Mr Hardcastle's; (*Winking upon the* LANDLORD.) Mr Hardcastle's, of Quag-mire Marsh, you understand me.

LANDLORD. Master Hardcastle's! Lock-a-daisy, my masters, you're come a deadly deal wrong! When you came to the bottom of the hill, you should have crossed down Squash Lane.

MARLOW. Cross down Squash Lane!

LANDLORD. Then you were to keep straight forward, till you came to four roads.

MARLOW. Come to where four roads meet!

TONY. Ay; but you must be sure to take only one of them.

MARLOW. O sir, you're facetious.

TONY. Then keeping to the right, you are to go sideways till
you come upon Crack-skull Common: there you must look
sharp for the track of the wheel, and go forward, till you
come to farmer Murrain's barn. Coming to the farmer's
barn, you are to turn to the right, and then to the left, and
then to the right about again, till you find out the old mill –

MARLOW. Zounds, man! we could as soon find out the
longitude!

HASTINGS. What's to be done, Marlow?

MARLOW. This house promises but a poor reception; though
perhaps the Landlord can accommodate us.

LANDLORD. Alack, master, we have but one spare bed in the
whole house.

TONY. And to my knowledge, that's taken up by three lodgers
already. (*After a pause, in which the rest seem disconcerted.*) I have
hit it. Don't you think, Stingo, our landlady could
accommodate the gentlemen by the fire-side, with – three
chairs and a bolster?

HASTINGS. I hate sleeping by the fire-side.

MARLOW. And I detest your three chairs and a bolster.

TONY. You do, do you? – then let me see – what – if you go
on a mile further, to the Buck's Head; the old Buck's Head
on the hill, one of the best inns in the whole county?

HASTINGS. O ho! so we have escaped an adventure for this
night, however.

LANDLORD (*apart to* TONY). Sure, you ben't sending them to
your father's as an inn, be you?

TONY. Mum, you fool you. Let *them* find that out. (*To them.*)
You have only to keep on straight forward, till you come to

a large old house by the roadside. You'll see a pair of large horns over the door. That's the sign. Drive up the yard, and call stoutly about you.

HASTINGS. Sir, we are obliged to you. The servants can't miss the way?

TONY. No, no: But I must tell you though, the landlord is rich, and going to leave off business; so he wants to be thought a gentleman, saving your presence, he! he! he! He'll be for giving you his company, and ecod if you mind him, he'll persuade you that his mother was an alderman, and his aunt a Justice of Peace.

LANDLORD. A troublesome old blade to be sure; but a keeps as good wines and beds as any in the whole country.

MARLOW. Well, if he supplies us with these, we shall want no further connection. We are to turn to the right, did you say?

TONY. No, no; straight forward. I'll just step myself, and show you a piece of the way. (*To the* LANDLORD.) Mum.

LANDLORD Ah, bless your heart for a sweet, pleasant – damned mischievous son of a whore.

Exeunt.

Act II

Scene. An old-fashioned house.

Enter HARDCASTLE, *followed by three or four awkward* SERVANTS.

HARDCASTLE. Well, I hope you're perfect in the table exercise I have been teaching you these three days. You all know your posts and your places, and can show that you have been used to good company, without ever stirring from home.

[ALL]. Ay, ay.

HARDCASTLE. When company comes, you are not to pop out and stare, and then run in again, like frighted rabbits in a warren.

[ALL]. No, no.

HARDCASTLE. You, Diggory, whom I have taken from the barn, are to make a show at the side-table; and you, Roger, whom I have advanced from the plough, are to place yourself behind *my* chair. But you're not to stand so, with your hands in your pockets. Take your hands from your pockets, Roger; and from your head, you blockhead you. See how Diggory carries his hands. They're a little too stiff, indeed, but that's no great matter.

DIGGORY. Ay, mind how I hold them. I learned to hold my hands this way, when I was upon drill for the militia. And so being upon drill –

HARDCASTLE. You must not be so talkative, Diggory. You must be all attention to the guests. You must hear us talk, and not think of talking; you must see us drink, and not think of drinking; you must see us eat, and not think of eating.

DIGGORY. By the laws, your worship, that's parfectly unpossible. When ever Diggory sees yeating going forward, ecod he's always wishing for a mouthful himself.

HARDCASTLE. Blockhead! Is not a belly-full in the kitchen as good as a belly-full in the parlour? Stay your stomach with that reflection.

DIGGORY. Ecod I thank your worship, I'll make a shift to stay my stomach with a slice of cold beef in the pantry.

HARDCASTLE. Diggory, you are too talkative. Then if I happen to say a good thing, or tell a good story at table, you must not all burst out a-laughing, as if you made part of the company.

DIGGORY. Then ecod your worship must not tell the story of Ould Grouse in the gun-room: I can't help laughing at that – he! he! he! – for the soul of me. We have laughed at that these twenty years – ha! ha! ha!

HARDCASTLE. Ha! ha! ha! The story is a good one. Well, honest Diggory, you may laugh at that – but still remember to be attentive. Suppose one of the company should call for a glass of wine, how will you behave? A glass of wine, sir, if you please (*To* DIGGORY.) – Eh, why don't you move?

DIGGORY. Ecod, your worship, I never have courage till I see the eatables and drinkables brought upo' the table, and then I'm as bauld as a lion.

HARDCASTLE. What, will nobody move?

FIRST SERVANT. I'm not to leave this pleace.

SECOND SERVANT. I'm sure it's no pleace of mine.

THIRD SERVANT. Nor mine, for sartain.

DIGGORY. Wauns, and I'm sure it canna be mine.

HARDCASTLE. You numbskulls! and so while, like your
betters, you are quarrelling for places, the guests must be
starved. Oh you dunces! I find I must begin all over again. –
But don't I hear a coach drive into the yard? To your posts,
you blockheads. I'll go in the meantime and give my old
friend's son a hearty reception at the gate.

Exit HARDCASTLE.

DIGGORY. By the elevens, my pleace is gone quite out of my
head.

ROGER. I know that my pleace is to be everywhere.

FIRST SERVANT Where the devil is mine?

SECOND SERVANT. My pleace is to be nowhere at all; and
so Ize go about my business.

Exeunt SERVANTS, *running about as if frighted, different ways.*

Enter SERVANT *with candles, showing in* MARLOW *and*
HASTINGS.

SERVANT. Welcome, gentlemen, very welcome. This way.

HASTINGS. After the disappointments of the day, welcome
once more, Charles, to the comforts of a clean room and a
good fire. Upon my word, a very well-looking house; antique,
but creditable.

MARLOW. The usual fate of a large mansion. Having first
ruined the master by good housekeeping, it at last comes to
levy contributions as an inn.

HASTINGS. As you say, we passengers are to be taxed to pay
all these fineries. I have often seen a good sideboard, or a

marble chimneypiece, though not actually put in the bill, inflame a reckoning confoundedly.

MARLOW. Travellers, George, must pay in all places. The only difference is, that in good inns, you pay dearly for luxuries; in bad ones, you are fleeced and starved.

HASTINGS. You have lived pretty much among them. In truth, I have been often surprised, that you who have seen so much of the world, with your natural good sense, and your many opportunities, could never yet acquire a requisite share of assurance.

MARLOW. The Englishman's malady. But tell me, George, where could I have learned that assurance you talk of? My life has been chiefly spent in a college, or an inn, in seclusion from that lovely part of the creation that chiefly teach men confidence. I don't know that I was ever familiarly acquainted with a single modest woman – except my mother – But among females of another class you know –

HASTINGS. Ay, among them you are impudent enough of all conscience.

MARLOW. They are of *us* you know.

HASTINGS. But in the company of women of reputation I never saw such an idiot, such a trembler; you look for all the world as if you wanted an opportunity of stealing out of the room.

MARLOW. Why man that's because I *do* want to steal out of the room. Faith, I have often formed a resolution to break the ice, and rattle away at any rate. But I don't know how, a single glance from a pair of fine eyes has totally overset my resolution. An impudent fellow may counterfeit modesty, but I'll be hanged if a modest man can ever counterfeit impudence.

HASTINGS. If you could but say half the fine things to them that I have heard you lavish upon the barmaid of an inn, or even a college bedmaker –

MARLOW. Why, George, I can't say fine things to them. They freeze, they petrify me. They may talk of a comet, or a burning mountain, or some such bagatelle. But to me, a modest woman, dressed out in all her finery, is the most tremendous object of the whole creation.

HASTINGS. Ha! ha! ha! At this rate, man, how can you ever expect to marry!

MARLOW. Never, unless as among kings and princes, my bride were to be courted by proxy. If, indeed, like an Eastern bridegroom, one were to be introduced to a wife he never saw before, it might be endured. But to go through all the terrors of a formal courtship, together with the episode of aunts, grandmothers, and cousins, and at last to blurt out the broad staring question, of, 'Madam, will you marry me?' No, no, that's a strain much above me I assure you.

HASTINGS. I pity you. But how do you intend behaving to the lady you are come down to visit at the request of your father?

MARLOW. As I behave to all other ladies. Bow very low. Answer yes, or no, to all her demands – But for the rest, I don't think I shall venture to look in her face, till I see my father's again.

HASTINGS. I'm surprised that one who is so warm a friend can be so cool a lover.

MARLOW. To be explicit, my dear Hastings, my chief inducement down was to be instrumental in forwarding your happiness, not my own. Miss Neville loves you, the family don't know you, as my friend you are sure of a reception, and let honour do the rest.

HASTINGS. My dear Marlow! But I'll suppress the emotion. Were I a wretch, meanly seeking to carry off a fortune, you should be the last man in the world I would apply to for assistance. But Miss Neville's person is all I ask, and that is mine, both from her deceased father's consent, and her own inclination.

MARLOW. Happy man! You have talents and art to captivate any woman. I'm doomed to adore the sex, and yet to converse with the only part of it I despise. This stammer in my address, and this awkward prepossessing visage of mine, can never permit me to soar above the reach of a milliner's 'prentice, or one of the duchesses of Drury Lane. Pshaw! this fellow here to interrupt us.

Enter HARDCASTLE.

HARDCASTLE. Gentlemen, once more you are heartily welcome. Which is Mr Marlow? Sir, you're heartily welcome. It's not my way, you see, to receive my friends with my back to the fire. I like to give them a hearty reception in the old style at my gate. I like to see their horses and trunks taken care of.

MARLOW (*aside*). He has got our names from the servants already. (*To him.*) We approve your caution and hospitality, sir. (*To* HASTINGS.) I have been thinking, George, of changing our travelling dresses in the morning. I am grown confoundedly ashamed of mine.

HARDCASTLE. I beg, Mr Marlow, you'll use no ceremony in this house.

HASTINGS. I fancy, Charles, you're right: the first blow is half the battle. I intend opening the campaign with the white and gold.

HARDCASTLE. Mr Marlow – Mr Hastings – gentlemen – pray be under no constraint in this house. This is Liberty-Hall, gentlemen. You may do just as you please here.

MARLOW. Yet, George, if we open the campaign too fiercely at first, we may want ammunition before it is over. I think to reserve the embroidery to secure a retreat.

HARDCASTLE. Your talking of a retreat, Mr Marlow, puts me in mind of the Duke of Marlborough, when we went to besiege Denain. He first summoned the garrison.

MARLOW. Don't you think the *ventre d'or* waistcoat will do with the plain brown?

HARDCASTLE. He first summoned the garrison, which might consist of about five thousand men –

HASTINGS. I think not: brown and yellow mix but very poorly.

HARDCASTLE. I say, gentlemen, as I was telling you, he summoned the garrison, which might consist of about five thousand men –

MARLOW. The girls like finery.

HARDCASTLE. Which might consist of about five thousand men, well appointed with stores, ammunition, and other implements of war. Now, says the Duke of Marlborough, to George Brooks, that stood next to him – You must have heard of George Brooks; I'll pawn my Dukedom, says he, but I take that garrison without spilling a drop of blood. So –

MARLOW. What, my good friend, if you gave us a glass of punch in the meantime, it would help us to carry on the siege with vigour.

HARDCASTLE. Punch, sir! (*Aside.*) This is the most unaccountable kind of modesty I ever met with.

MARLOW. Yes, sir, punch. A glass of warm punch, after our journey, will be comfortable. This is Liberty-Hall, you know.

HARDCASTLE. Here's Cup, sir.

MARLOW (*aside*). So this fellow, in his Liberty-Hall, will only let us have just what he pleases.

HARDCASTLE (*taking the cup*). I hope you'll find it to your mind. I have prepared it with my own hands, and I believe you'll own the ingredients are tolerable. Will you be so good as to pledge me, sir? Here, Mr Marlow, here is to our better acquaintance. (*Drinks.*)

MARLOW (*aside*). A very impudent fellow this! but he's a character, and I'll humour him a little. Sir, my service to you. (*Drinks.*)

HASTINGS (*aside*). I see this fellow wants to give us his company, and forgets that he's an inn-keeper, before he has learned to be a gentleman.

MARLOW. From the excellence of your Cup, my old friend, I suppose you have a good deal of business in this part of the country. Warm work, now and then, at elections, I suppose.

HARDCASTLE. No, sir, I have long given that work over. Since our betters have hit upon the expedient of electing each other, there's no business for us that sell ale.

HASTINGS. So, then you have no turn for politics I find.

HARDCASTLE. Not in the least. There was a time, indeed, I fretted myself about the mistakes of government, like other people; but finding myself every day grow more angry, and the government growing no better, I left it to mend itself. Since that, I no more trouble my head about Hyder Ali, or Ali Khan, than about Ally Croaker. Sir, my service to you.

HASTINGS. So that with eating above stairs, and drinking below, with receiving your friends within and amusing them without, you lead a good pleasant bustling life of it.

HARDCASTLE. I do stir about a great deal, that's certain. Half the differences of the parish are adjusted in this very parlour.

MARLOW (*after drinking*). And you have an argument in your cup, old gentleman, better than any in Westminster-Hall.

HARDCASTLE. Ay, young gentleman, that, and a little philosophy.

MARLOW (*aside*). Well, this is the first time I ever heard of an innkeeper's philosophy.

HASTINGS. So then, like an experienced general, you attack them on every quarter. If you find their reason manageable, you attack it with your philosophy; if you find they have no reason, you attack them with this. Here's your health, my philosopher. (*Drinks.*)

HARDCASTLE. Good, very good, thank you; ha, ha. Your Generalship puts me in mind of Prince Eugene, when he fought the Turks at the battle of Belgrade. You shall hear.

MARLOW. Instead of the battle of Belgrade, I believe it's almost time to talk about supper. What has your philosophy got in the house for supper?

HARDCASTLE. For supper, sir! (*Aside.*) Was ever such a request to a man in his own house!

MARLOW. Yes, sir, supper sir; I begin to feel an appetite. I shall make devilish work tonight in the larder, I promise you.

HARDCASTLE (*aside*). Such a brazen dog sure never my eyes beheld. (*To him.*) Why really, sir, as for supper I can't well tell. My Dorothy, and the cookmaid, settle these things between them. I leave these kind of things entirely to them.

MARLOW. You do, do you?

HARDCASTLE. Entirely. By-the-bye, I believe they are in actual consultation upon what's for supper this moment in the kitchen.

MARLOW. Then I beg they'll admit *me* as one of their privy council. It's a way I have got. When I travel, I always choose to regulate my own supper. Let the cook be called. No offence I hope, sir.

HARDCASTLE. O no, sir, none in the least; yet I don't know how: our Bridget, the cookmaid, is not very communicative upon these occasions. Should we send for her, she might scold us all out of the house.

HASTINGS. Let's see your list of the larder then. I ask it as a favour. I always match my appetite to my bill of fare.

MARLOW (*to* HARDCASTLE, *who looks at them with surprise*). Sir, he's very right, and it's my way too.

HARDCASTLE. Sir, you have a right to command here. Here, Roger, bring us the bill of fare for tonight's supper. I believe it's drawn out. Your manner, Mr Hastings, puts me in mind of my uncle, Colonel Wallop. It was a saying of his, that no man was sure of his supper till he had eaten it.

[*Enter* ROGER, *with a Bill of Fare.*]

HASTINGS (*aside*). All upon the high ropes! His uncle a Colonel! We shall soon hear of his mother being a Justice of Peace. But let's hear the bill of fare.

MARLOW (*perusing*). What's here? For the first course; for the second course; for the dessert. The devil, sir, do you think we have brought down the whole Joiners Company, or the Corporation of Bedford, to eat up such a supper? Two or three little things, clean and comfortable, will do.

HASTINGS. But, let's hear it.

MARLOW (*reading*). For the first course at the top, a pig, and prune sauce.

HASTINGS. Damn your pig, I say.

MARLOW. And damn your prune sauce, say I.

HARDCASTLE. And yet, gentlemen, to men that are hungry, pig with prune sauce, is very good eating.

MARLOW. At the bottom, a calf's tongue and brains.

HASTINGS. Let your brains be knocked out, my good sir; I don't like them.

MARLOW. Or you may clap them on a plate by themselves. I do.

HARDCASTLE (*aside*). Their impudence confounds me. (*To them.*) Gentlemen, you are my guests, make what alterations you please. Is there anything else you wish to retrench or alter, gentlemen?

MARLOW. Item. A pork pie, a boiled rabbit and sausages, a florentine, a shaking pudding, and a dish of tiff-taff-taffety cream!

HASTINGS. Confound your made dishes, I shall be as much at a loss in this house as at a green and yellow dinner at the French ambassador's table. I'm for plain eating.

HARDCASTLE. I'm sorry, gentlemen, that I have nothing you like, but if there be anything you have a particular fancy to –

MARLOW. Why, really, sir, your bill of fare is so exquisite, that any one part of it is full as good as another. Send us what you please. So much for supper. And now to see that our beds are aired, and properly taken care of.

HARDCASTLE. I entreat you'll leave all that to me. You shall not stir a step.

MARLOW. Leave that to you! I protest, sir, you must excuse me, I always look to these things myself.

HARDCASTLE. I must insist, sir, you'll make yourself easy on that head.

MARLOW. You see I'm resolved on it. (*Aside.*) A very troublesome fellow this, as ever I met with.

HARDCASTLE. Well, sir, I'm resolved at least to attend you. (*Aside.*) This may be modern modesty, but I never saw anything look so like old-fashioned impudence.

Exeunt MARLOW *and* HARDCASTLE.

HASTINGS. So I find this fellow's civilities begin to grow troublesome. But who can be angry at those assiduities which are meant to please him? Ha! what do I see? Miss Neville, by all that's happy!

Enter MISS NEVILLE.

MISS NEVILLE. My dear Hastings! To what unexpected good fortune? to what accident am I to ascribe this happy meeting?

HASTINGS. Rather let me ask the same question, as I could never have hoped to meet my dearest Constance at an inn.

MISS NEVILLE. An inn! sure you mistake! my aunt, my guardian, lives here. What could induce you to think this house an inn?

HASTINGS. My friend Mr Marlow, with whom I came down, and I, have been sent here as to an inn, I assure you. A young fellow whom we accidentally met at a house hard by directed us hither.

MISS NEVILLE. Certainly it must be one of my hopeful cousin's tricks, of whom you have heard me talk so often, ha! ha! ha! ha!

HASTINGS. He whom your aunt intends for you? He of whom I have such just apprehensions?

MISS NEVILLE. You have nothing to fear from him, I assure you. You'd adore him if you knew how heartily he despises me. My aunt knows it too, and has undertaken to court me for him, and actually begins to think she has made a conquest.

HASTINGS. Thou dear dissembler! You must know, my Constance, I have just seized this happy opportunity of my friend's visit here to get admittance into the family. The horses that carried us down are now fatigued with their journey, but they'll soon be refreshed; and then if my dearest girl will trust in her faithful Hastings, we shall soon be landed in France, where even among slaves the laws of marriage are respected.

MISS NEVILLE. I have often told you, that though ready to obey you, I yet should leave my little fortune behind with reluctance. The greatest part of it was left me by my uncle, the India Director, and chiefly consists in jewels. I have been for some time persuading my aunt to let me wear them. I fancy I'm very near succeeding. The instant they are put into my possession you shall find me ready to make them and myself yours.

HASTINGS. Perish the baubles! Your person is all I desire. In the meantime, my friend Marlow must not be let into his mistake. I know the strange reserve of his temper is such, that if abruptly informed of it, he would instantly quit the house before our plan was ripe for execution.

MISS NEVILLE. But how shall we keep him in the deception? Miss Hardcastle is just returned from walking; what if we still continue to deceive him? – This, this way –

They confer. Enter MARLOW.

MARLOW. The assiduities of these good people tease me beyond bearing. My host seems to think it ill manners to leave me alone, and so he claps not only himself but his old-fashioned wife on my back. They talk of coming to sup with us too; and then, I suppose, we are to run the gauntlet through all the rest of the family. – What have we got here!

HASTINGS. My dear Charles! Let me congratulate you! – The most fortunate accident! – Who do you think is just alighted?

MARLOW. Cannot guess.

HASTINGS. Our mistresses boy, Miss Hardcastle and Miss Neville. Give me leave to introduce Miss Constance Neville to your acquaintance. Happening to dine in the neighbourhood, they called on their return to take fresh horses here. Miss Hardcastle has just stepped into the next room, and will be back in an instant. Wasn't it lucky? eh?

MARLOW (*aside*). I have just been mortified enough of all conscience, and here comes something to complete my embarrassment.

HASTINGS. Well! but wasn't it the most fortunate thing in the world?

MARLOW. Oh! yes. Very fortunate – a most joyful encounter – But our dresses, George, you know, are in disorder – What if we should postpone the happiness till tomorrow? – Tomorrow at her own house – It will be every bit as convenient – And rather more respectful – Tomorrow let it be.

Offering to go.

MISS NEVILLE. By no means, sir. Your ceremony will displease her. The disorder of your dress will show the ardour of your impatience. Besides, she knows you are in the house, and will permit you to see her.

MARLOW. Oh! the devil! how shall I support it? Hem! hem! Hastings, you must not go. You are to assist me, you know. I shall be confoundedly ridiculous. Yet, hang it! I'll take courage. Hem!

HASTINGS. Pshaw man! it's but the first plunge, and all's over. She's but a woman, you know.

MARLOW. And of all women, she that I dread most to encounter!

Enter MISS HARDCASTLE *as returned from walking, with a bonnet, etc.*

HASTINGS (*introducing them*). Miss Hardcastle, Mr Marlow, I'm proud of bringing two persons of such merit together, that only want to know, to esteem each other.

MISS HARDCASTLE (*aside*). Now, for meeting my modest gentleman with a demure face, and quite in his own manner. (*After a pause, in which he appears very uneasy and disconcerted.*) I'm glad of your safe arrival, sir – I'm told you had some accidents by the way.

MARLOW. Only a few madam. Yes we had some. Yes, madam, a good many accidents, but should be sorry – madam – or rather glad of any accidents – that are so agreeably concluded. Hem!

HASTINGS (*to him*). You never spoke better in your whole life. Keep it up, and I'll ensure you the victory.

MISS HARDCASTLE. I'm afraid you flatter, sir. You that have seen so much of the finest company can find little entertainment in an obscure corner of the country.

MARLOW (*gathering courage*). I have lived, indeed, in the world, madam; but I have kept very little company. I have been but an observer upon life, madam, while others were enjoying it.

MISS NEVILLE. But that, I am told, is the way to enjoy it at last.

HASTINGS (*to him*). Cicero never spoke better. Once more, and you are confirmed in assurance for ever.

MARLOW (*to him*). Hem! Stand by me then, and when I'm down, throw in a word or two to set me up again.

MISS HARDCASTLE. An observer, like you, upon life, were, I fear, disagreeably employed, since you must have had much more to censure than to approve.

MARLOW. Pardon me, madam. I was always willing to be amused. The folly of most people is rather an object of mirth than uneasiness.

HASTINGS (*to him*). Bravo, Bravo. Never spoke so well in your whole life. Well! Miss Hardcastle, I see that you and Mr Marlow are going to be very good company. I believe our being here will but embarrass the interview.

MARLOW. Not in the least, Mr Hastings. We like your company of all things. (*To him.*) Zounds! George, sure you won't go? How can you leave us?

HASTINGS. Our presence will but spoil conversation, so we'll retire to the next room. (*To him.*) You don't consider, man, that we are to manage a little tête-à-tête of our own.

Exeunt HASTINGS *and* MISS NEVILLE.

MISS HARDCASTLE (*after a pause*). But you have not been wholly an observer, I presume, sir: the ladies I should hope have employed some part of your addresses.

MARLOW (*relapsing into timidity*). Pardon me, madam, I – I – I – As yet have studied – only – to – deserve them.

MISS HARDCASTLE. And that some say is the very worst way to obtain them.

MARLOW. Perhaps so, madam. But I love to converse only with the more grave and sensible part of the sex. – But I'm afraid I grow tiresome.

MISS HARDCASTLE. Not at all, sir; there is nothing I like so much as grave conversation myself; I could hear it for ever. Indeed I have often been surprised how a man of sentiment could ever admire those light airy pleasures, where nothing reaches the heart.

MARLOW. It's – a disease – of the mind, madam. In the variety of tastes there must be some who wanting a relish – for – um – a – um.

MISS HARDCASTLE. I understand you, sir. There must be some, who wanting a relish for refined pleasures, pretend to despise what they are incapable of tasting.

MARLOW. My meaning, madam, but infinitely better expressed. And I can't help observing – a –

MISS HARDCASTLE (aside). Who could ever suppose this fellow impudent upon some occasions? (To him.) You were going to observe, sir –

MARLOW. I was observing, madam – I protest, madam, I forget what I was going to observe.

MISS HARDCASTLE (aside). I vow and so do I. (To him.) You were observing, sir, that in this age of hypocrisy – something about hypocrisy, sir.

MARLOW. Yes, madam. In this age of hypocrisy there are few who upon strict enquiry do not – a – a – a –

MISS HARDCASTLE. I understand you perfectly, sir.

MARLOW (aside). Egad! and that's more than I do myself.

MISS HARDCASTLE. You mean that in this hypocritical age there are few that do not condemn in public what they practise in private, and think they pay every debt to virtue when they praise it.

MARLOW. True, madam; those who have most virtue in their mouths, have least of it in their bosoms. But I'm sure I tire you, madam.

MISS HARDCASTLE. Not in the least, sir; there's something so agreeable and spirited in your manner, such life and force – pray, sir, go on.

MARLOW. Yes, madam. I was saying – that there are some occasions – when a total want of courage, madam, destroys all the – and puts us – upon a – a – a –

MISS HARDCASTLE. I agree with you entirely, a want of courage upon some occasions assumes the appearance of ignorance, and betrays us when we most want to excel. I beg you'll proceed.

MARLOW. Yes, madam. Morally speaking, madam – but I see Miss Neville expecting us in the next room. I would not intrude for the world.

MISS HARDCASTLE. I protest, sir, I never was more agreeably entertained in all my life. Pray go on.

MARLOW. Yes, madam. I was – But she beckons us to join her. Madam, shall I do myself the honour to attend you?

MISS HARDCASTLE. Well then, I'll follow.

MARLOW (*aside*). This pretty smooth dialogue has done for me.

Exit.

MISS HARDCASTLE. Ha! ha! ha! Was there ever such a sober sentimental interview? I'm certain he scarce looked in my face the whole time. Yet the fellow, but for his unaccountable bashfulness, is pretty well too. He has good sense, but then so buried in his fears, that it fatigues one more than ignorance. If I could teach him a little confidence, it would be doing somebody that I know of a piece of service. But who is that somebody? – that, faith, is a question I can scarce answer.

Exit.

Enter TONY *and* MISS NEVILLE, *followed by* MRS HARDCASTLE *and* HASTINGS.

TONY. What do you follow me for, cousin Con? I wonder you're not ashamed to be so very engaging.

MISS NEVILLE. I hope, cousin, one may speak to one's own relations, and not be to blame.

TONY. Ay, but I know what sort of a relation you want to make me though; but it won't do. I tell you, cousin Con, it won't do, so I beg you'll keep your distance, I want no nearer relationship.

She follows coqueting him to the Back Scene.

MRS HARDCASTLE. Well! I vow, Mr Hastings, you are very entertaining. There's nothing in the world I love to talk of so much as London, and the fashions, though I was never there myself.

HASTINGS. Never there! You amaze me! From your air and manner, I concluded you had been bred all your life either at Ranelagh, St James's, or Tower Wharf.

MRS HARDCASTLE. Oh! Sir, you're only pleased to say so. We country persons can have no manner at all. I'm in love with the town, and that serves to raise me above some of our neighbouring rustics; but who can have a manner, that has never seen the Pantheon, the Grotto Gardens, the Borough, and such places where the Nobility chiefly resort?

All I can do, is to enjoy London at second-hand. I take care to know every tête-à-tête from the *Scandalous Magazine*, and have all the fashions, as they come out, in a letter from the two Miss Rickets of Crooked Lane. Pray how do you like this head, Mr Hastings?

HASTINGS. Extremely elegant and *dégagée*, upon my word, madam. Your *Friseur* is a Frenchman, I suppose?

MRS HARDCASTLE. I protest I dressed it myself from a print in the *Ladies Memorandum-book* for the last year.

HASTINGS. Indeed. Such a head in a side-box, at the Playhouse, would draw as many gazers as my Lady Mayoress at a City Ball.

MRS HARDCASTLE. I vow, since inoculation began, there is no such thing to be seen as a plain woman; so one must dress a little particular or one may escape in the crowd.

HASTINGS. But that can never be your case, madam, in any dress.

Bowing.

MRS HARDCASTLE. Yet, what signifies *my* dressing when I have such a piece of antiquity by my side as Mr Hardcastle: all I can say will never argue down a single button from his clothes. I have often wanted him to throw off his great flaxen wig, and where he was bald, to plaster it over like my Lord Pately, with powder.

HASTINGS. You are right, madam; for, as among the ladies, there are none ugly, so among the men there are none old.

MRS HARDCASTLE. But what do you think his answer was? Why, with his usual Gothic vivacity, he said I only wanted him to throw off his wig to convert it into a *tête* for my own wearing.

HASTINGS. Intolerable! At your age you may wear what you
please, and it must become you.

MRS HARDCASTLE. Pray, Mr Hastings, what do you take to
be the most fashionable age about town?

HASTINGS. Some time ago, forty was all the mode; but I'm
told the ladies intend to bring up fifty for the ensuing winter.

MRS HARDCASTLE. Seriously? Then I shall be too young
for the fashion.

HASTINGS. No lady begins now to put on jewels till she's past
forty. For instance, Miss there, in a polite circle, would be
considered as a child, as a mere maker of samplers.

MRS HARDCASTLE. And yet Mrs Niece thinks herself as
much a woman, and is as fond of jewels as the oldest of us
all.

HASTINGS. Your niece, is she? And that young gentleman, a
brother of yours, I should presume?

MRS HARDCASTLE. My son, sir. They are contracted to
each other. Observe their little sports. They fall in and out
ten times a day, as if they were man and wife already. (*To
them.*) Well Tony, child, what soft things are you saying to
your cousin Constance this evening?

TONY. I have been saying no soft things; but that it's very
hard to be followed about so. Ecod! I've not a place in the
house now that's left to myself but the stable.

MRS HARDCASTLE. Never mind him, Con my dear. He's in
another story behind your back.

MISS NEVILLE. There's something generous in my cousin's
manner. He falls out before faces to be forgiven in private.

TONY. That's a damned confounded – crack.

MRS HARDCASTLE. Ah! he's a sly one. Don't you think they're like each other about the mouth, Mr Hastings? The Blenkinsop mouth to a T. They're of a size too. Back to back, my pretties, that Mr Hastings may see you. Come Tony.

TONY. You had as good not make me, I tell you. (*Measuring.*)

MISS NEVILLE. O lud! he has almost cracked my head.

MRS HARDCASTLE. Oh the monster! For shame, Tony. You a man, and behave so!

TONY. If I'm a man, let me have my fortin. Ecod! I'll not be made a fool of no longer.

MRS HARDCASTLE. Is this, ungrateful boy, all that I'm to get for the pains I have taken in your education? I that have rocked you in your cradle, and fed that pretty mouth with a spoon! Did not I work that waistcoat to make you genteel? Did not I prescribe for you every day, and weep while the receipt was operating?

TONY. Ecod! you had reason to weep, for you have been dosing me ever since I was born. I have gone through every receipt in the *Complete Huswife* ten times over; and you have thoughts of coursing me through *Quincy* next spring. But, ecod! I tell you, I'll not be made a fool of no longer.

MRS HARDCASTLE. Wasn't it all for your good, viper? Wasn't it all for your good?

TONY. I wish you'd let me and my good alone then. Snubbing this way when I'm in spirits. If I'm to have any good, let it come of itself; not to keep dinging it, dinging it into one so.

MRS HARDCASTLE. That's false; I never see you when you're in spirits. No, Tony, you then go to the alehouse or kennel. I'm never to be delighted with your agreeable, wild notes, unfeeling monster!

TONY. Ecod! Mama, your own notes are the wildest of the two.

MRS HARDCASTLE. Was ever the like? But I see he wants to break my heart, I see he does.

HASTINGS. Dear madam, permit me to lecture the young gentleman a little. I'm certain I can persuade him to his duty.

MRS HARDCASTLE. Well! I must retire. Come, Constance, my love. You see Mr Hastings, the wretchedness of my situation: was ever poor woman so plagued with a dear, sweet, pretty, provoking, undutiful boy.

Exeunt MRS HARDCASTLE *and* MISS NEVILLE.

TONY (*singing*). 'There was a young man riding by, and fain would have his will. Rang do didlo dee.' Don't mind her. Let her cry. It's the comfort of her heart. I have seen her and sister cry over a book for an hour together, and they said, they liked the book the better the more it made them cry.

HASTINGS. Then you're no friend to the ladies, I find, my pretty young gentleman?

TONY. That's as I find 'm.

HASTINGS. Not to her of your mother's choosing, I dare answer? And yet she appears to me a pretty well-tempered girl.

TONY. That's because you don't know her as well as I. Ecod! I know every inch about her; and there's not a more bitter cantankerous toad in all Christendom.

HASTINGS (*aside*). Pretty encouragement this for a lover!

TONY. I have seen her since the height of that. She has as many tricks as a hare in a thicket, or a colt the first day's breaking.

HASTINGS. To me she appears sensible and silent!

TONY. Ay, before company. But when she's with her playmates she's as loud as a hog in a gate.

HASTINGS. But there is a meek modesty about her that charms me.

TONY. Yes, but curb her never so little, she kicks up, and you're flung in a ditch.

HASTINGS. Well, but you must allow her a little beauty. – Yes, you must allow her some beauty.

TONY. Bandbox! She's all a made up thing, mun. Ah! could you but see Bet Bouncer of these parts, you might then talk of beauty. Ecod, she has two eyes as black as sloes, and cheeks as broad and red as a pulpit cushion. She'd make two of she.

HASTINGS. Well, what say you to a friend that would take this bitter bargain off your hands?

TONY. Anon?

HASTINGS. Would you thank him that would take Miss Neville and leave you to happiness and your dear Betsy?

TONY. Ay; but where is there such a friend, for who would take *her?*

HASTINGS. I am he. If you but assist me, I'll engage to whip her off to France, and you shall never hear more of her.

TONY. Assist you! Ecod I will, to the last drop of my blood. I'll clap a pair of horses to your chaise that shall trundle you off in a twinkling, and maybe get you a part of her fortin beside, in jewels, that you little dream of.

HASTINGS. My dear squire, this looks like a lad of spirit.

TONY. Come along then, and you shall see more of my spirit before you have done with me. (*Singing.*) 'We are the boys that fears no noise where the thundering cannons roar.'

Exeunt.

Act III

Enter HARDCASTLE.

HARDCASTLE. What could my old friend Sir Charles mean
by recommending his son as the modestest young man in
town? To me he appears the most impudent piece of brass
that ever spoke with a tongue. He has taken possession of
the easy chair by the fireside already. He took off his boots
in the parlour, and desired me to see them taken care of. I'm
desirous to know how his impudence affects my daughter. –
She will certainly be shocked at it.

Enter MISS HARDCASTLE, *plainly dressed*.

Well, my Kate, I see you have changed your dress as I bid
you; and yet, I believe, there was no great occasion.

MISS HARDCASTLE. I find such a pleasure, sir, in obeying
your commands, that I take care to observe them without
ever debating their propriety.

HARDCASTLE. And yet, Kate, I sometimes give you some
cause, particularly when I recommended my *modest* gentleman to you as a lover today.

MISS HARDCASTLE. You taught me to expect something
extraordinary, and I find the original exceeds the description.

HARDCASTLE. I was never so surprised in my life! He has
quite confounded all my faculties!

MISS HARDCASTLE. I never saw anything like it: and a man
of the world too!

HARDCASTLE. Ay, he learned it all abroad, – what a fool was I, to think a young man could learn modesty by travelling. He might as soon learn wit at a masquerade.

MISS HARDCASTLE. It seems all natural to him.

HARDCASTLE. A good deal assisted by bad company and a French dancing-master.

MISS HARDCASTLE. Sure you mistake, papa! a French dancing-master could never have taught him that timid look, – that awkward address, – that bashful manner –

HARDCASTLE. Whose look? whose manner? child!

MISS HARDCASTLE. Mr Marlow's: his *mauvaise honte*, his timidity, struck me at the first sight.

HARDCASTLE. Then your first sight deceived you; for I think him one of the most brazen first sights that ever astonished my senses.

MISS HARDCASTLE. Sure, sir, you rally! I never saw anyone so modest.

HARDCASTLE. And can you be serious! I never saw such a bouncing swaggering puppy since I was born. Bully Dawson was but a fool to him.

MISS HARDCASTLE. Surprising! He met me with a respect-ful bow, a stammering voice, and a look fixed on the ground.

HARDCASTLE. He met me with loud voice, a lordly air, and a familiarity that made my blood freeze again.

MISS HARDCASTLE. He treated me with diffidence and respect; censured the manners of the age; admired the prudence of girls that never laughed; tired me with apologies for being tiresome; then left the room with a bow, and, madam, I would not for the world detain you.

HARDCASTLE. He spoke to me as if he knew me all his life before. Asked twenty questions, and never waited for an answer. Interrupted my best remarks with some silly pun, and when I was in my best story of the Duke of Marlborough and Prince Eugene, he asked if I had not a good hand at making punch. Yes, Kate, he asked your father if he was a maker of punch!

MISS HARDCASTLE. One of us must certainly be mistaken.

HARDCASTLE. If he be what he has shown himself, I'm determined he shall never have my consent.

MISS HARDCASTLE. And if he be the sullen thing I take him, he shall never have mine.

HARDCASTLE. In one thing then we are agreed – to reject him.

MISS HARDCASTLE. Yes. But upon conditions. For if you should find him less impudent, and I more presuming; if you find him more respectful, and I more importunate – I don't know – the fellow is well enough for a man – certainly we don't meet many such at a horse race in the country.

HARDCASTLE. If we should find him so – but that's impossible. The first appearance has done my business. I'm seldom deceived in that.

MISS HARDCASTLE. And yet there may be many good qualities under that first appearance.

HARDCASTLE. Ay, when a girl finds a fellow's outside to her taste, she then sets about guessing the rest of his furniture. With her, a smooth face stands for good sense, and a genteel figure for every virtue.

MISS HARDCASTLE. I hope, sir, a conversation begun with a compliment to my good sense won't end with a sneer at my understanding?

HARDCASTLE. Pardon me, Kate. But if young Mr Brazen
can find the art of reconciling contradictions, he may please
us both, perhaps.

MISS HARDCASTLE. And as one of us must be mistaken,
what if we go to make further discoveries?

HARDCASTLE. Agreed. But depend on't I'm in the right.

MISS HARDCASTLE. And depend on't I'm not much in the
wrong.

Exeunt. Enter TONY *running in with a casket.*

TONY. Ecod! I have got them. Here they are. My cousin
Con's necklaces, bobs and all. My mother shan't cheat the
poor souls out of their fortune neither. Oh! my genus, is that
you?

Enter HASTINGS.

HASTINGS. My dear friend, how have you managed with
your mother? I hope you have amused her with pretending
love for your cousin, and that you are willing to be
reconciled at last? Our horses will be refreshed in a short
time, and we shall soon be ready to set off.

TONY. And here's something to bear your charges by the way.
(*Giving the casket.*) Your sweetheart's jewels. Keep them, and
hang those, I say, that would rob you of one of them.

HASTINGS. But how have you procured them from your
mother?

TONY. Ask me no questions, and I'll tell you no fibs. I procured them by the rule of thumb. If I had not a key to
every drawer in mother's bureau, how could I go to the
alehouse so often as I do? An honest man may rob himself
of his own at any time.

HASTINGS. Thousands do it every day. But to be plain with you; Miss Neville is endeavouring to procure them from her aunt this very instant. If she succeeds, it will be the most delicate way at least of obtaining them.

TONY. Well, keep them, till you know how it will be. But I know how it will be well enough, she'd as soon part with the only sound tooth in her head.

HASTINGS. But I dread the effects of her resentment, when she finds she has lost them.

TONY. Never you mind her resentment, leave *me* to manage that. I don't value her resentment the bounce of a cracker. Zounds! here they are. Morris. Prance.

Exit HASTINGS.

Enter MRS HARDCASTLE, MISS NEVILLE.

MRS HARDCASTLE. Indeed, Constance, you amaze me. Such a girl as you want jewels? It will be time enough for jewels, my dear, twenty years hence, when your beauty begins to want repairs.

MISS NEVILLE. But what will repair beauty at forty, will certainly improve it at twenty, madam.

MRS HARDCASTLE. Yours, my dear, can admit of none. That natural blush is beyond a thousand ornaments. Besides, child, jewels are quite out at present. Don't you see half the ladies of our acquaintance, my Lady Killdaylight, and Mrs Crump, and the rest of them, carry their jewels to town, and bring nothing but paste and marcasites back.

MISS NEVILLE. But who knows, madam, but somebody that shall be nameless would like me best with all my little finery about me?

MRS HARDCASTLE. Consult your glass, my dear, and then see, if with such a pair of eyes, you want any better sparklers. What do you think, Tony, my dear, does your cousin Con want any jewels, in your eyes, to set off her beauty?

TONY. That's as thereafter may be.

MISS NEVILLE. My dear aunt, if you knew how it would oblige me.

MRS HARDCASTLE. A parcel of old-fashioned rose- and table-cut things. They would make you look like the court of King Solomon at a puppet-show. Besides, I believe I can't readily come at them. They may be missing for ought I know to the contrary.

TONY (*apart to* MRS HARDCASTLE). Then why don't you tell her so at once, as she's so longing for them. Tell her they're lost. It's the only way to quiet her. Say they're lost, and call me to bear witness.

MRS HARDCASTLE (*apart to* TONY). You know, my dear, I'm only keeping for you. So if I say they're gone, you'll bear me witness, will you? He! he! he!

TONY. Never fear me. Ecod! I'll say I saw them taken out with my own eyes.

MISS NEVILLE. I desire them but for a day, madam. Just to be permitted to show them as relics, and then they may be locked up again.

MRS HARDCASTLE. To be plain with you, my dear Constance; if I could find them, you should have them. They're missing, I assure you. Lost, for ought I know; but we must have patience wherever they are.

MISS NEVILLE. I'll not believe it; this is but a shallow pretence to deny me. I know they're too valuable to be so slightly kept, and as you are to answer for the loss.

MRS HARDCASTLE. Don't be alarmed, Constance. If they be lost, I must restore an equivalent. But my son knows they are missing, and not to be found.

TONY. That I can bear witness to. They are missing, and not to be found, I'll take my oath on't.

MRS HARDCASTLE. You must learn resignation, my dear; for though we lose our fortune, yet we should not lose our patience. See me, how calm I am.

MISS NEVILLE. Ay, people are generally calm at the misfortunes of others.

MRS HARDCASTLE. Now, I wonder a girl of your good sense should waste a thought upon such trumpery. We shall soon find them; and, in the meantime, you shall make use of my garnets till your jewels be found.

MISS NEVILLE. I detest garnets.

MRS HARDCASTLE. The most becoming things in the world to set off a clear complexion. You have often seen how well they look upon me. You *shall* have them.

Exit.

MISS NEVILLE. I dislike them of all things. You shan't stir. – Was ever anything so provoking to mislay my own jewels, and force me to wear her trumpery?

TONY. Don't be a fool. If she gives you the garnets, take what you can get. The jewels are your own already. I have stolen them out of her bureau, and she does not know it. Fly to your spark, he'll tell you more of the matter. Leave me to manage *her.*

MISS NEVILLE. My dear cousin.

[*Exit.*]

TONY. Vanish. She's here, and has missed them already. Zounds! how she fidgets and spits about like a Catharine wheel.

Enter MRS HARDCASTLE.

MRS HARDCASTLE. Confusion! thieves! robbers! We are cheated, plundered, broke open, undone.

TONY. What's the matter, what's the matter, mama? I hope nothing has happened to any of the good family!

MRS HARDCASTLE. We are robbed. My bureau has been broke open, the jewels taken out, and I'm undone.

TONY. Oh! is that all? Ha! ha! ha! By the laws, I never saw it better acted in my life. Ecod, I thought you was ruined in earnest, ha! ha! ha!

MRS HARDCASTLE. Why boy, I *am* ruined in earnest. My bureau has been broke open, and all taken away.

TONY. Stick to that; ha! ha! ha! Stick to that. I'll bear witness, you know, call me to bear witness.

MRS HARDCASTLE. I tell you, Tony, by all that's precious, the jewels are gone, and I shall be ruined for ever.

TONY. Sure I know they're gone, and I am to say so.

MRS HARDCASTLE. My dearest Tony, but hear me. They're gone, I say.

TONY. By the laws, mama, you make me for to laugh, ha! ha! I know who took them well enough, ha! ha! ha!

MRS HARDCASTLE. Was there ever such a blockhead, that can't tell the difference between jest and earnest? I tell you I'm not in jest, booby.

TONY. That's right, that's right: you must be in a bitter passion, and then nobody will suspect either of us. I'll bear witness that they are gone.

MRS HARDCASTLE. Was there ever such a cross-grained
brute, that won't hear me! Can you bear witness that you're
no better than a fool! Was ever poor woman so beset with
fools on one hand, and thieves on the other?

TONY. I can bear witness to that.

MRS HARDCASTLE. Bear witness again, you blockhead you,
and I'll turn you out of the room directly. My poor niece,
what will become of *her!* Do you laugh, you unfeeling brute,
as if you enjoyed my distress?

TONY. I can bear witness to that.

MRS HARDCASTLE. Do you insult me, monster? I'll teach
you to vex your mother, I will.

TONY. I can bear witness to that.

He runs off, she follows him. Enter MISS HARDCASTLE *and*
MAID.

MISS HARDCASTLE. What an unaccountable creature is that
brother of mine, to send them to the house as an inn, ha!
ha! I don't wonder at his impudence.

MAID. But what is more, madam, the young gentleman, as
you passed by in your present dress, asked me, if you were
the barmaid? He mistook you for the barmaid, madam.

MISS HARDCASTLE. Did he? Then as I live I'm resolved to
keep up the delusion. Tell me, Pimple, how do you like my
present dress? Don't you think I look something like Cherry
in *The Beaux' Stratagem?*

MAID. It's the dress, madam, that every lady wears in the
country, but when she visits or receives company.

MISS HARDCASTLE. And are you sure he does not
remember my face or person?

MAID. Certain of it.

MISS HARDCASTLE. I vow I thought so; for though we spoke for some time together, yet his fears were such, that he never once looked up during the interview. Indeed, if he had, my bonnet would have kept him from seeing me.

MAID. But what do you hope from keeping him in his mistake?

MISS HARDCASTLE. In the first place, I shall be *seen*, and that is no small advantage to a girl who brings her face to market. Then I shall perhaps make an acquaintance, and that's no small victory gained over one who never addresses any but the wildest of her sex. But my chief aim is to take my gentleman off his guard, and like an invisible champion of romance examine the giant's force before I offer to combat.

MAID. But are you sure you can act your part, and disguise your voice, so that he may mistake that, as he has already mistaken your person?

MISS HARDCASTLE. Never fear me. I think I have got the true bar cant. – Did your honour call? – Attend the Lion there. – Pipes and tobacco for the Angel. – The Lamb has been outrageous this half hour.

MAID. It will do, madam. But he's here.

Exit MAID. *Enter* MARLOW.

MARLOW. What a bawling in every part of the house; I have scarce a moment's repose. If I go to the best room, there I find my host and his story. If I fly to the gallery, there we have my hostess with her curtsey down to the ground. I have at last got a moment to myself, and now for recollection.

Walks and muses.

MISS HARDCASTLE. Did you call, sir? Did your honour call?

MARLOW (*musing*). As for Miss Hardcastle, she's too grave and sentimental for me.

MISS HARDCASTLE. Did your honour call?

She still places herself before him, he turning away.

MARLOW. No, child. (*Musing.*) Besides from the glimpse I had of her, I think she squints.

MISS HARDCASTLE. I'm sure, sir, I heard the bell ring.

MARLOW. No, no. (*Musing.*) I have pleased my father, however, by coming down, and I'll tomorrow please myself by returning.

Taking out his tablets, and perusing.

MISS HARDCASTLE. Perhaps the other gentleman called, sir.

MARLOW. I tell you, no.

MISS HARDCASTLE. I should be glad to know, sir. We have such a parcel of servants.

MARLOW. No, no, I tell you. (*Looks full in her face.*) Yes, child, I think I did call. I wanted – I wanted – I vow, child, you are vastly handsome.

MISS HARDCASTLE. O la, sir, you'll make one ashamed.

MARLOW. Never saw a more sprightly malicious eye. Yes, yes, my dear, I did call. Have you got any of your – a – what-d'ye-call-it in the house?

MISS HARDCASTLE. No, sir, we have been out of that these ten days.

MARLOW. One may call in this house, I find, to very little purpose. Suppose I should call for a taste, just by way of trial, of the nectar of your lips; perhaps I might be disappointed of that too.

MISS HARDCASTLE. Nectar! nectar! that's a liquor there's no call for in these parts. French, I suppose. We keep no French wines here, sir.

MARLOW. Of true English growth, I assure you.

MISS HARDCASTLE. Then it's odd I should not know it. We brew all sorts of wines in this house, and I have lived here these eighteen years.

MARLOW. Eighteen years! Why one would think, child, you kept the bar before you were born. How old are you?

MISS HARDCASTLE. Oh! sir, I must not tell my age. They say women and music should never be dated.

MARLOW. To guess at this distance, you can't be much above forty. (*Approaching*). Yet nearer I don't think so much. (*Approaching.*) By coming close to some women they look younger still; but when we come very close indeed – (*Attempting to kiss her.*)

MISS HARDCASTLE. Pray, sir, keep your distance. One would think you wanted to know one's age as they do horses, by mark of mouth.

MARLOW. I protest, child, you use me extremely ill. If you keep me at this distance, how is it possible you and I can be ever acquainted?

MISS HARDCASTLE. And who wants to be acquainted with you? I want no such acquaintance, not I. I'm sure you did not treat Miss Hardcastle that was here a while ago in this obstropalous manner. I'll warrant me, before her you looked

dashed, and kept bowing to the ground, and talked, for all
the world, as if you was before a Justice of Peace.

MARLOW (*aside*). Egad! she has hit it, sure enough. (*To her.*) In
awe of her, child? Ha! ha! ha! A mere, awkward, squinting
thing, no, no. I find you don't know me. I laughed, and
rallied her a little; but I was unwilling to be too severe. No,
I could not be too severe, curse me!

MISS HARDCASTLE. Oh! then, sir, you are a favourite, I
find, among the ladies?

MARLOW. Yes, my dear, a great favourite. And yet, hang me,
I don't see what they find in me to follow. At the Ladies
Club in town, I'm called their agreeable Rattle. Rattle, child,
is not my real name, but one I'm known by. My name is
Solomons. Mr Solomons, my dear, at your service.

Offering to salute her.

MISS HARDCASTLE. Hold, sir; you were introducing me to
your club, not to yourself. And you're so great a favourite
there you say?

MARLOW. Yes, my dear. There's Mrs Mantrap, Lady Betty
Blackleg, the Countess of Sligo, Mrs Langhorns, old Miss
Biddy Buckskin, and your humble servant, keep up the spirit
of the place.

MISS HARDCASTLE. Then it's a very merry place, I suppose.

MARLOW. Yes, as merry as cards, suppers, wine, and old
women can make us.

MISS HARDCASTLE. And their agreeable Rattle, ha! ha! ha!

MARLOW (*aside*). Egad! I don't quite like this chit. She looks
knowing, methinks. You laugh, child!

MISS HARDCASTLE. I can't but laugh to think what time
they all have for minding their work or their family.

MARLOW (*aside*). All's well, she don't laugh at me. (*To her.*)
Do *you* ever work, child?

MISS HARDCASTLE. Ay, sure. There's not a screen or a
quilt in the whole house but what can bear witness to that.

MARLOW. Odso! Then you must show me your embroidery.
I embroider and draw patterns myself a little. If you want a
judge of your work you must apply to me.

Seizing her hand.

MISS HARDCASTLE. Ay, but the colours don't look well by
candlelight. You shall see all in the morning.

Struggling.

MARLOW. And why not now, my angel? Such beauty fires
beyond the power of resistance. – Pshaw! the father here!
My old luck: I never nicked seven that I did not throw ames
ace three times following.

Exit MARLOW. *Enter* HARDCASTLE, *who stands in surprise.*

HARDCASTLE. So, madam! So I find *this* is your *modest* lover.
This is your humble admirer that kept his eyes fixed on the
ground, and only adored at humble distance. Kate, Kate,
art thou not ashamed to deceive your father so?

MISS HARDCASTLE. Never trust me, dear papa, but he's
still the modest man I first took him for, you'll be convinced
of it as well as I.

HARDCASTLE. By the hand of my body I believe his
impudence is infectious! Didn't I see him seize your hand?
Didn't I see him haul you about like a milkmaid? and now
you talk of his respect and his modesty, forsooth!

MISS HARDCASTLE. But if I shortly convince you of his
modesty, that he has only the faults that will pass off with

time, and the virtues that will improve with age, I hope you'll forgive him.

HARDCASTLE. The girl would actually make one run mad! I tell you I'll not be convinced. I am convinced. He has scarcely been three hours in the house, and he has already encroached on all my prerogatives. You may like his impudence, and call it modesty. But my son-in-law, madam, must have very different qualifications.

MISS HARDCASTLE. Sir, I ask but this night to convince you.

HARDCASTLE. You shall not have half the time, for I have thoughts of turning him out this very hour.

MISS HARDCASTLE. Give me that hour then, and I hope to satisfy you.

HARDCASTLE. Well, an hour let it be then. But I'll have no trifling with your father. All fair and open, do you mind me?

MISS HARDCASTLE. I hope, sir, you have ever found that I considered your commands as my pride; for your kindness is such, that my duty as yet has been inclination.

Exeunt.

Act IV

Enter HASTINGS *and* MISS NEVILLE.

HASTINGS. You surprise me! Sir Charles Marlow expected here this night? Where have you had your information?

MISS NEVILLE. You may depend upon it. I just saw his letter to Mr Hardcastle, in which he tells him he intends setting out a few hours after his son.

HASTINGS. Then, my Constance, all must be completed before he arrives. He knows me; and should he find me here, would discover my name, and perhaps my designs, to the rest of the family.

MISS NEVILLE. The jewels, I hope, are safe.

HASTINGS. Yes, yes. I have sent them to Marlow, who keeps the keys of our baggage. In the meantime, I'll go to prepare matters for our elopement. I have had the Squire's promise of a fresh pair of horses; and, if I should not see him again, will write him further directions.

Exit.

MISS NEVILLE. Well! success attend you. In the meantime, I'll go amuse my aunt with the old pretence of a violent passion for my cousin.

Exit. Enter MARLOW, *followed by a* SERVANT.

MARLOW. I wonder what Hastings could mean by sending me so valuable a thing as a casket to keep for him, when he knows the only place I have is the seat of a post-coach at an inn-door. Have you deposited the casket with the landlady, as I ordered you? Have you put it into her own hands?

SERVANT. Yes, your honour.

MARLOW. She said she'd keep it safe, did she?

SERVANT. Yes, she said she'd keep it safe enough; she asked me, how I came by it? and she said she had a great mind to make me give an account of myself.

Exit SERVANT.

MARLOW. Ha! ha! ha! They're safe however. What an unaccountable set of beings have we got amongst! This little barmaid though runs in my head most strangely, and drives out the absurdities of all the rest of the family. She's mine, she must be mine, or I'm greatly mistaken.

Enter HASTINGS.

HASTINGS. Bless me! I quite forgot to tell her that I intended to prepare at the bottom of the garden. Marlow here, and in spirits too!

MARLOW. Give me joy, George! Crown me, shadow me with laurels! Well, George, after all, we modest fellows don't want for success among the women.

HASTINGS. Some women you mean. But what success has your honour's modesty been crowned with now, that it grows so insolent upon us?

MARLOW. Didn't you see the tempting, brisk, lovely, little thing that runs about the house with a bunch of keys to its girdle?

HASTINGS. Well! and what then?

MARLOW. She's mine, you rogue you. Such fire, such motion, such eyes, such lips – but, egad! she would not let me kiss them though.

HASTINGS. But are you so sure, so very sure of her?

MARLOW. Why man, she talked of showing me her work above-stairs, and I am to improve the pattern.

HASTINGS. But how can *you*, Charles, go about to rob a woman of her honour?

MARLOW. Pshaw! pshaw! we all know the honour of the barmaid of an inn. I don't intend to *rob* her, take my word for it, there's nothing in this house, I shan't honestly *pay* for.

HASTINGS. I believe the girl has virtue.

MARLOW. And if she has, I should be the last man in the world that would attempt to corrupt it.

HASTINGS. You have taken care, I hope, of the casket I sent you to lock up? It's in safety?

MARLOW. Yes yes. It's safe enough. I have taken care of it. But how could you think the seat of a post-coach at an inn-door a place of safety? Ah! numbskull! I have taken better precautions for you than you did for yourself. – I have –

HASTINGS. What!

MARLOW. I have sent it to the landlady to keep for you.

HASTINGS. To the landlady!

MARLOW. The landlady.

HASTINGS. You did.

MARLOW. I did. She's to be answerable for its forthcoming, you know.

HASTINGS. Yes, she'll bring it forth, with a witness.

MARLOW. Wasn't I right? I believe you'll allow that I acted prudently upon this occasion?

HASTINGS (*aside*). He must not see my uneasiness.

MARLOW. You seem a little disconcerted though, methinks. Sure nothing has happened?

HASTINGS. No, nothing. Never was in better spirits in all my life. And so you left it with the landlady who, no doubt, very readily undertook the charge?

MARLOW. Rather too readily. For she not only kept the casket; but, through her great precaution, was going to keep the messenger too. Ha! ha! ha!

HASTINGS. He! he! he! They're safe however.

MARLOW. As a guinea in a miser's purse.

HASTINGS (*aside*). So now all hopes of fortune are at an end, and we must set off without it. (*To him.*) Well, Charles, I'll leave you to your meditations on the pretty barmaid, and, he! he! he! may you be as successful for yourself as you have been for me.

Exit.

MARLOW. Thank ye, George! I ask no more. Ha! ha! ha!

Enter HARDCASTLE.

HARDCASTLE. I no longer know my own house. It's turned all topsy-turvy. His servants have got drunk already. I'll bear it no longer, and yet, from my respect for his father, I'll be calm. (*To him.*) Mr Marlow, your servant, I'm your very humble servant.

Bowing low.

MARLOW. Sir, your humble servant. (*Aside.*) What's to be the wonder now?

HARDCASTLE. I believe, sir, you must be sensible, sir, that no man alive ought to be more welcome than your father's son, sir. I hope you think so?

MARLOW. I do from my soul, sir. I don't want much entreaty. I generally make my father's son welcome wherever he goes.

HARDCASTLE. I believe you do, from my soul, sir. But though I say nothing to your own conduct, that of your servants is insufferable. Their manner of drinking is setting a very bad example in this house, I assure you.

MARLOW. I protest, my very good sir, that's no fault of mine. If they don't drink as they ought *they* are to blame. I ordered them not to spare the cellar. I did, I assure you. (*To the side scene.*) Here, let one of my servants come up. (*To him.*) My positive directions were, that as I did not drink myself, they should make up for my deficiencies below.

HARDCASTLE. Then they had your orders for what they do! I'm satisfied!

MARLOW. They had, I assure you. You shall hear from one of themselves.

Enter SERVANT *drunk.*

MARLOW. You, Jeremy! Come forward, sirrah! What were my orders? Were you not told to drink freely, and call for what you thought fit, for the good of the house?

HARDCASTLE (*aside*). I begin to lose my patience.

SERVANT. Please your honour, liberty and Fleet Street for ever! Though I'm but a servant, I'm as good as another man. I'll drink for no man before supper, sir, damme! Good liquor will sit upon a good supper, but a good supper will not sit upon – hiccup – upon my conscience, sir.

MARLOW. You see, my old friend, the fellow is as drunk as he can possibly be. I don't know what you'd have more, unless you'd have the poor devil soused in a beer-barrel.

HARDCASTLE. Zounds! He'll drive me distracted if I contain

myself any longer. Mr Marlow. Sir; I have submitted to your insolence for more than four hours, and I see no likelihood of its coming to an end. I'm now resolved to be master here, sir, and I desire that you and your drunken pack may leave my house directly.

MARLOW. Leave your house! – Sure you jest, my good friend? What, when I'm doing what I can to please you?

HARDCASTLE. I tell you, sir, you don't please me; so I desire you'll leave my house.

MARLOW. Sure you cannot be serious? At this time o'night, and such a night. You only mean to banter me?

HARDCASTLE. I tell you, sir, I'm serious; and, now that my passions are roused, I say this house is mine, sir; this house is mine, and I command you to leave it directly.

MARLOW. Ha! ha! ha! A puddle in a storm. I shan't stir a step, I assure you. (*In a serious tone.*) This, your house, fellow! It's my house. This is my house. Mine, while I choose to stay. What right have you to bid me leave this house, sir? I never met with such impudence, curse me, never in my whole life before.

HARDCASTLE. Nor I, confound me if ever I did. To come to my house, to call for what he likes, to turn me out of my own chair, to insult the family, to order his servants to get drunk, and then to tell me, 'This house is mine, sir.' By all that's impudent it makes me laugh. Ha! ha! ha! Pray, sir, (*Bantering.*) as you take the house, what think you of taking the rest of the furniture? There's a pair of silver candlesticks, and there's a fire-screen, and here's a pair of brazen-nosed bellows, perhaps you may take a fancy to them?

MARLOW. Bring me your bill, sir, bring me your bill, and let's make no more words about it.

HARDCASTLE. There are a set of prints too. What think you of the *Rake's Progress* for your own apartment?

MARLOW. Bring me your bill, I say; and I'll leave you and your infernal house directly.

HARDCASTLE. Then there's a mahogany table, that you may see your own face in.

MARLOW. My bill, I say.

HARDCASTLE. I had forgot the great chair, for your own particular slumbers, after a hearty meal.

MARLOW. Zounds! bring me my bill, I say, and let's hear no more on't.

HARDCASTLE. Young man, young man, from your father's letter to me, I was taught to expect a well-bred modest man as a visitor here, but now I find him no better than a coxcomb and a bully; but he will be down here presently, and shall hear more of it.

Exit.

MARLOW. How's this! Sure I have not mistaken the house! Everything looks like an inn. The servants cry, 'Coming'. The attendance is awkward; the barmaid too to attend us. But she's here, and will further inform me. Whither so fast, child? A word with you.

Enter MISS HARDCASTLE.

MISS HARDCASTLE. Let it be short then. I'm in a hurry. (*Aside.*) I believe he begins to find out his mistake, but it's too soon quite to undeceive him.

MARLOW. Pray, child, answer me one question. What are you, and what may your business in this house be?

MISS HARDCASTLE. A relation of the family, sir.

MARLOW. What? A poor relation?

MISS HARDCASTLE. Yes, sir. A poor relation appointed to keep the keys, and to see that the guests want nothing in my power to give them.

MARLOW. That is, you act as the barmaid of this inn.

MISS HARDCASTLE. Inn! O law – What brought that in your head? One of the best families in the county keep an inn! Ha! ha! ha! old Mr Hardcastle's house an inn!

MARLOW. Mr Hardcastle's house! Is this house Mr Hardcastle's house, child!

MISS HARDCASTLE. Ay, sure. Whose else should it be?

MARLOW. So then all's out, and I have been damnably imposed on. Oh, confound my stupid head, I shall be laughed at over the whole town. I shall be stuck up in *caricatura* in all the print-shops. The *Dullissimo Macaroni*. To mistake this house of all others for an inn, and my father's old friend for an inn-keeper. What a swaggering puppy must he take me for. What a silly puppy do I find myself. There again, may I be hanged, my dear, but I mistook you for the barmaid.

MISS HARDCASTLE. Dear me! dear me! I'm sure there's nothing in my behaviour to put me upon a level with one of that stamp.

MARLOW. Nothing, my dear, nothing. But I was in for a list of blunders, and could not help making you a subscriber. My stupidity saw everything the wrong way. I mistook your assiduity for assurance, and your simplicity for allurement. But it's over – This house I no more show *my* face in.

MISS HARDCASTLE. I hope, sir, I have done nothing to disoblige you. I'm sure I should be sorry to affront any gentleman who has been so polite, and said so many civil things to me. I'm sure I should be sorry (*Pretending to cry.*) if he left the family upon my account. I'm sure I should be sorry people said anything amiss, since I have no fortune but my character.

MARLOW (*aside*). By heaven, she weeps. This is the first mark of tenderness I ever had from a modest woman, and it touches me; (*To her*) excuse me, my lovely girl, you are the only part of the family I leave with reluctance. But to be plain with you, the difference of our birth, fortune, and education, make an honourable connection impossible; and I can never harbour a thought of seducing simplicity that trusted in my honour, or bringing ruin upon one, whose only fault was being too lovely.

MISS HARDCASTLE (*aside*). Generous man! I now begin to admire him. (*To him.*) But I'm sure my family is as good as Miss Hardcastle's, and though I'm poor, that's no great misfortune to a contented mind, and, until this moment, I never thought that it was bad to want fortune.

MARLOW. And why now, my pretty simplicity?

MISS HARDCASTLE. Because it puts me at a distance from one, that if I had a thousand pound I would give it all too.

MARLOW (*aside*). This simplicity bewitches me, so that if I stay I'm undone. I must make one bold effort, and leave her. (*To her.*) Your partiality in my favour, my dear, touches me most sensibly, and were I to live for myself alone, I could easily fix my choice. But I owe too much to the opinion of the world, too much to the authority of a father, so that – I can scarcely speak it – it affects me. Farewell.

Exit.

MISS HARDCASTLE. I never knew half his merit till now. He shall not go, if I have power or art to detain him. I'll still preserve the character in which I stooped to conquer, but will undeceive my papa, who, perhaps, may laugh him out of his resolution.

Exit. Enter TONY, MISS NEVILLE.

TONY. Ay, you may steal for yourselves the next time. I have done my duty. She has got the jewels again, that's a sure thing; but she believes it was all a mistake of the servants.

MISS NEVILLE. But, my dear cousin, sure you won't forsake us in this distress? If she in the least suspects that I am going off, I shall certainly be locked up, or sent to my aunt Pedigree's, which is ten times worse.

TONY. To be sure, aunts of all kinds are damned bad things. But what can I do? I have got you a pair of horses that will fly like Whistlejacket, and I'm sure you can't say but I have courted you nicely before her face. Here she comes, we must court a bit or two more, for fear she should suspect us.

They retire, and seem to fondle. Enter MRS HARDCASTLE.

MRS HARDCASTLE. Well, I was greatly fluttered, to be sure. But my son tells me it was all a mistake of the servants. I shan't be easy, however, till they are fairly married, and then let her keep her own fortune. But what do I see! Fondling together, as I'm alive. I never saw Tony so sprightly before. Ah! have I caught you, my pretty doves! What, billing, exchanging stolen glances, and broken murmurs? Ah!

TONY. As for murmurs, mother, we grumble a little now and then, to be sure. But there's no love lost between us.

MRS HARDCASTLE. A mere sprinkling, Tony, upon the flame, only to make it burn brighter.

MISS NEVILLE. Cousin Tony promises to give us more of his company at home. Indeed, he shan't leave us any more. It won't leave us cousin Tony, will it?

TONY. Oh! it's a pretty creature. No, I'd sooner leave my horse in a pound, than leave you when you smile upon one so. Your laugh makes you so becoming.

MISS NEVILLE. Agreeable cousin! Who can help admiring that natural humour, that pleasant, broad, red, thoughtless, (*Patting his cheek.*) ah! it's a bold face.

MRS HARDCASTLE. Pretty innocence.

TONY. I'm sure I always loved cousin Con's hazel eyes, and her pretty long fingers, that she twists this way and that, over the haspicholls, like a parcel of bobbins.

MRS HARDCASTLE. Ah, he would charm the bird from the tree. I was never so happy before. My boy takes after his father, poor Mr Lumpkin, exactly. The jewels, my dear Con, shall be yours incontinently. You shall have them. Isn't he a sweet boy, my dear? You shall be married tomorrow, and we'll put off the rest of his education, like Dr Drowsy's sermons, to a fitter opportunity.

Enter DIGGORY.

DIGGORY. Where's the Squire? I have got a letter for your worship.

TONY. Give it to my mama. She reads all my letters first.

DIGGORY. I had orders to deliver it into your own hands.

TONY. Who does it come from?

DIGGORY. Your worship mun ask that o' the letter itself.

TONY. I could wish to know, though.

Turning the letter, and gazing on it.

MISS NEVILLE (*aside*). Undone, undone. A letter to him from Hastings. I know the hand. If my aunt sees it, we are ruined for ever. I'll keep her employed a little if I can.

(*To* MRS HARDCASTLE.) But I have not told you, madam, of my cousin's smart answer just now to Mr Marlow. We so laughed – You must know, madam – this way a little, for he must not hear us.

They confer.

TONY (*still gazing*). A damned cramp piece of penmanship, as ever I saw in my life. I can read your print-hand very well. But here there are such handles, and shanks, and dashes, that one can scarce tell the head from the tail. 'To Anthony Lumpkin, Esquire.' It's very odd, I can read the outside of my letters, where my own name is, well enough. But when I come to open it, it's all-buzz. That's hard, very hard; for the inside of the letter is always the cream of the correspondence.

MRS HARDCASTLE. Ha! ha! ha! Very well, very well. And so my son was too hard for the philosopher.

MISS NEVILLE. Yes, madam; but you must hear the rest, madam. A little more this way, or he may hear us. You'll hear how he puzzled him again.,

MRS HARDCASTLE. He seems strangely puzzled now himself, methinks.

TONY (*still gazing*). A damned up and down hand, as if it was disguised in liquor. (*Reading.*) 'Dear Sir.' Ay, that's that. Then there's an 'M', and a 'T', and an 'S', but whether the next be an 'izzard' or an 'R', confound me, I cannot tell.

MRS HARDCASTLE. What's that, my dear? Can I give you any assistance?

MISS NEVILLE. Pray, aunt, let me read it. Nobody reads a cramp hand better than I. (*Twitching the letter from her.*) Do you know who it is from?

TONY. Can't tell, except from Dick Ginger the feeder.

MISS NEVILLE. Ay, so it is, (*Pretending to read.*) 'Dear Squire, Hoping that you're in health, as I am at this present. The gentlemen of the Shake-bag club has cut the gentlemen of Goose-green quite out of feather. The odds – um – odd battle – um – long fighting' – um – here, here, it's all about cocks, and fighting; it's of no consequence, here, put it up, put it up.

Thrusting the crumpled letter upon him.

TONY. But I tell you, Miss, it's of all the consequence in the world. I would not lose the rest of it for a guinea. Here, mother, do you make it out. Of no consequence!

Giving MRS HARDCASTLE *the letter.*

MRS HARDCASTLE. How's this! (*Reads.*) 'Dear Squire, I'm now waiting for Miss Neville, with a post-chaise and pair, at the bottom of the garden, but I find my horses yet unable to perform the journey. I expect you'll assist us with a pair of fresh horses, as you promised. Dispatch is necessary, as the *hag* (ay the hag) your mother, will otherwise suspect us. Yours, Hastings.' Grant me patience! I shall run distracted! My rage chokes me!

MISS NEVILLE. I hope, madam, you'll suspend your resentment for a few moments, and not impute to me any impertinence, or sinister design that belongs to another.

MRS HARDCASTLE (*curtseying very low*). Fine spoken, madam, you are most miraculously polite and engaging, and quite the very pink of courtesy and circumspection, madam. (*Changing her tone.*) And you, you great ill-fashioned oaf with scarce sense enough to keep your mouth shut. Were you too joined against me? But I'll defeat all your plots in a moment. As for you, madam, since you have got a pair of fresh horses ready, it would be cruel to disappoint them. So, if you please, instead of running away with your spark, prepare, this very moment, to run off with *me*. Your old aunt Pedigree will keep you secure, I'll warrant me. You too, sir, may mount your horse, and guard us upon the way. Here, Thomas, Roger, Diggory. I'll show you that I wish you better than you do yourselves.

Exit.

MISS NEVILLE. So now I'm completely ruined.

TONY. Ay, that's a sure thing.

MISS NEVILLE. What better could be expected from being connected with such a stupid fool, and after all the nods and signs I made him.

TONY. By the laws, Miss, it was your own cleverness, and not my stupidity, that did your business. You were so nice and so busy with your Shake-bags and Goose-greens, that I thought you could never be making believe.

Enter HASTINGS.

HASTINGS. So, sir, I find by my servant, that you have shown my letter, and betrayed us. Was this well done, young gentleman?

TONY. Here's another. Ask Miss there who betrayed you. Ecod, it was her doing, not mine.

Enter MARLOW.

MARLOW. So I have been finely used here among you. Rendered contemptible, driven into ill manners, despised, insulted, laughed at.

TONY. Here's another. We shall have old Bedlam broke loose presently.

MISS NEVILLE. And there, sir, is the gentleman to whom we all owe every obligation.

MARLOW. What can I say to him, a mere boy, an idiot, whose ignorance and age are a protection?

HASTINGS. A poor contemptible booby, that would but disgrace correction.

MISS NEVILLE. Yet with cunning and malice enough to make himself merry with all our embarrassments.

HASTINGS. An insensible cub.

MARLOW. Replete with tricks and mischief.

TONY. Baw! damme, but I'll fight you both one after the other, – with baskets.

MARLOW. As for him, he's below resentment. But your conduct, Mr Hastings, requires an explanation. You knew of my mistakes, yet would not undeceive me.

HASTINGS. Tortured as I am with my own disappointments, is this a time for explanations! It is not friendly, Mr Marlow.

MARLOW. But sir –

MISS NEVILLE. Mr Marlow, we never kept on your mistake, till it was too late to undeceive you. Be pacified.

Enter SERVANT.

SERVANT. My mistress desires you'll get ready immediately, madam. The horses are putting to. Your hat and things are in the next room. We are to go thirty miles before morning.

Exit SERVANT.

MISS NEVILLE. Well, well; I'll come presently.

MARLOW (*to* HASTINGS). Was it well done, sir, to assist in rendering me ridiculous? To hang me out for the scorn of all my acquaintance? Depend upon it, sir, I shall expect an explanation.

HASTINGS. Was it well done, sir, if you're upon that subject, to deliver what I entrusted to yourself, to the care of another, sir?

MISS NEVILLE. Mr Hastings, Mr Marlow. Why will you increase my distress by this groundless dispute? I implore, I entreat you –

Enter SERVANT.

SERVANT. Your cloak, madam. My mistress is impatient.

MISS NEVILLE. I come. Pray be pacified. If I leave you thus, I shall die with apprehension.

Enter SERVANT.

SERVANT. Your fan, muff, and gloves, madam. The horses are waiting.

MISS NEVILLE. Oh, Mr Marlow! if you knew what a scene of constraint and ill-nature lies before me, I'm sure it would convert your resentment into pity.

MARLOW. I'm so distracted with a variety of passions, that I don't know what I do. Forgive me, madam. George, forgive me. You know my hasty temper, and should not exasperate it.

HASTINGS. The torture of my situation is my only excuse.

MISS NEVILLE. Well, my dear Hastings, if you have that esteem for me that I think, that I am sure you have, your constancy for three years will but increase the happiness of our future connection. If –

MRS HARDCASTLE (*within*). Miss Neville! Constance, why Constance, I say.

MISS NEVILLE. I'm coming. Well, constancy. Remember, constancy is the word.

Exit.

HASTINGS. My heart! How can I support this? To be so near happiness, and such happiness.

MARLOW (*to* TONY). You see now, young gentleman, the effects of your folly. What might be amusement to you, is here disappointment, and even distress.

TONY (*from a reverie*). Ecod, I have hit it. It's here. Your hands. Yours and yours, my poor Sulky. My boots there, ho! Meet me two hours hence at the bottom of the garden; and if you don't find Tony Lumpkin a more good-natured fellow than you thought for, I'll give you leave to take my best horse, and Bet Bouncer into the bargain. Come along. My boots, ho!

Exeunt.

Act V, Scene i

Scene continues.

Enter HASTINGS *and* SERVANT.

HASTINGS. You saw the old lady and Miss Neville drive off, you say.

SERVANT. Yes, your honour. They went off in a post coach, and the young Squire went on horseback. They're thirty miles off by this time.

HASTINGS. Then all my hopes are over.

SERVANT. Yes, sir. Old Sir Charles is arrived. He and the old gentleman of the house have been laughing at Mr Marlow's mistake this half hour. They are coming this way.

HASTINGS. Then I must not be seen. So now to my fruitless appointment at the bottom of the garden. This is about the time.

Exeunt. Enter SIR CHARLES *and* HARDCASTLE.

HARDCASTLE. Ha! ha! ha! The peremptory tone in which he sent forth his sublime commands.

SIR CHARLES. And the reserve with which I suppose he treated all your advances.

HARDCASTLE. And yet he might have seen something in me above a common inn-keeper, too.

SIR CHARLES. Yes, Dick, but he mistook you for an uncommon innkeeper, ha! ha! ha!

HARDCASTLE. Well, I'm in too good spirits to think of anything but joy. Yes, my dear friend, this union of our families will make our personal friendships hereditary; and though my daughter's fortune is but small –

SIR CHARLES. Why, Dick, will you talk of fortune to *me?* My son is possessed of more than a competence already, and can want nothing but a good and virtuous girl to share his happiness and increase it. If they like each other, as you say they do –

HARDCASTLE. *If*, man? I tell you they *do* like each other. My daughter as good as told me so.

SIR CHARLES. But girls are apt to flatter themselves, you know.

HARDCASTLE. I saw him grasp her hand in the warmest manner myself; and here he comes to put you out of your 'ifs', I warrant him.

Enter MARLOW.

MARLOW. I come, sir, once more, to ask pardon for my strange conduct. I can scarce reflect on my insolence without confusion.

HARDCASTLE. Tut, boy, a trifle. You take it too gravely. An hour or two's laughing with my daughter will set all to rights again. She'll never like you the worse for it.

MARLOW. Sir, I shall be always proud of her approbation.

HARDCASTLE. Approbation is but a cold word, Mr Marlow; if I am not deceived, you have something more than approbation thereabouts. You take me.

MARLOW. Really, sir, I have not that happiness.

HARDCASTLE. Come, boy, I'm an old fellow, and know what's what, as well as you that are younger. I know what has passed between you; but mum.

MARLOW. Sure, sir, nothing has passed between us but the most profound respect on my side, and the most distant reserve on hers. You don't think, sir, that my impudence has been passed upon all the rest of the family?

HARDCASTLE. Impudence! No, I don't say that – Not quite impudence – Though girls like to be played with, and rumpled a little too sometimes. But she has told no tales, I assure you.

MARLOW. I never gave her the slightest cause.

HARDCASTLE. Well, well, I like modesty in its place well enough. But this is over-acting, young gentleman. You *may* be open. Your father and I will like you the better for it.

MARLOW. May I die, sir, if I ever –

HARDCASTLE. I tell you, she don't dislike you; and as I'm sure you like her –

MARLOW. Dear sir – I protest, sir –

HARDCASTLE. I see no reason why you should not be joined as fast as the parson can tie you.

MARLOW. But hear me, sir –

HARDCASTLE. Your father approves the match, I admire it, every moment's delay will be doing mischief, so –

MARLOW. But why won't you hear me? By all that's just and true, I never gave Miss Hardcastle the slightest mark of my attachment, or even the most distant hint to suspect me of affection. We had but one interview, and that was formal, modest, and uninteresting.

HARDCASTLE (*aside*). This fellow's formal modest impudence is beyond bearing.

SIR CHARLES. And you never grasped her hand, or made any protestations!

MARLOW. As heaven is my witness, I came down in obedience to your commands. I saw the lady without emotion, and parted without reluctance. I hope you'll exact no further proofs of my duty, nor prevent me from leaving a house in which I suffer so many mortifications.

Exit.

SIR CHARLES. I'm astonished at the air of sincerity with which he parted.

HARDCASTLE. And I'm astonished at the deliberate intrepidity of his assurance.

SIR CHARLES. I dare pledge my life and honour upon his truth.

HARDCASTLE. Here comes my daughter, and I would stake my happiness upon her veracity.

Enter MISS HARDCASTLE.

HARDCASTLE. Kate, come hither, child. Answer us sincerely, and without reserve; has Mr Marlow made you any professions of love and affection.

MISS HARDCASTLE. The question is very abrupt, sir! But since you require unreserved sincerity, I think he has.

HARDCASTLE (*to* SIR CHARLES). You see.

SIR CHARLES. And pray, madam, have you and my son had more than one interview?

MISS HARDCASTLE. Yes, sir, several.

HARDCASTLE (*to* SIR CHARLES). You see.

SIR CHARLES. But did he profess any attachment?

MISS HARDCASTLE. A lasting one.

SIR CHARLES. Did he talk of love?

MISS HARDCASTLE. Much, sir.

SIR CHARLES. Amazing! And all this formally?

MISS HARDCASTLE. Formally.

HARDCASTLE. Now, my friend, I hope you are satisfied.

SIR CHARLES. And how did he behave, madam?

MISS HARDCASTLE. As most professed admirers do. Said
some civil things of my face, talked much of his want of
merit, and the greatness of mine; mentioned his heart, gave
a short tragedy speech, and ended with pretended rapture.

SIR CHARLES. Now I'm perfectly convinced, indeed. I know
his conversation among women to be modest and submissive.
This forward canting ranting manner by no means describes
him, and I am confident, he never sat for the picture.

MISS HARDCASTLE. Then what, sir, if I should convince
you to your face of my sincerity? If you and my papa, in
about half an hour, will I place yourselves behind that
screen, you shall hear him declare his passion to me in
person.

SIR CHARLES. Agreed. And if I find him what you describe,
all my happiness in him must have an end.

Exit.

MISS HARDCASTLE. And if you don't find him what I
describe – I fear my happiness must never have a beginning.

Exeunt.

Act V, Scene ii

Scene changes to the back of the garden.

Enter HASTINGS.

HASTINGS. What an idiot am I, to wait here for a fellow, who probably takes a delight in mortifying me. He never intended to be punctual, and I'll wait no longer. What do I see? It is he, and perhaps with news of my Constance.

Enter TONY, *booted and spattered.*

My honest Squire! I now find you a man of your word. This looks like friendship.

TONY. Ay, I'm your friend, and the best friend you have in the world, if you knew but all. This riding by night, by the bye, is cursedly tiresome. It has shook me worse than the basket of a stage-coach.

HASTINGS. But how? Where did you leave your fellow travellers? Are they in safety? Are they housed?

TONY. Five and twenty miles in two hours and a half is no such bad driving. The poor beasts have smoked for it: rabbit me, but I'd rather ride forty miles after a fox, than ten with such varment.

HASTINGS. Well, but where have you left the ladies? I die with impatience.

TONY. Left them? Why where should I leave them, but where I found them?

HASTINGS. This is a riddle.

TONY. Riddle me this then. What's that goes round the house, and round the house, and never touches the house?

HASTINGS. I'm still astray.

TONY. Why that's it, mon. I have led them astray. By jingo, there's not a pond or slough within five miles of the place but they can tell the taste of.

HASTINGS. Ha! ha! ha! I understand; you took them in a round, while they supposed themselves going forward. And so you have at last brought them home again.

TONY. You shall hear. I first took them down Feather-bed Lane, where we stuck fast in the mud. I then rattled them crack over the stones of Up-and-down Hill – I then introduced them to the gibbet on Heavy-tree Heath, and from that, with a circumbendibus, I fairly lodged them in the horsepond at the bottom of the garden.

HASTINGS. But no accident, I hope.

TONY. No, no. Only mother is confoundedly frightened. She thinks herself forty miles off. She's sick of the journey, and the cattle can scarce crawl. So if your own horses be ready, you may whip off with cousin, and I'll be bound that no soul here can budge a foot to follow you.

HASTINGS. My dear friend, how can I be grateful?

TONY. Ay, now it's dear friend, noble Squire. Just now, it was all idiot, cub, and run me through the guts. Damn *your* way of fighting, I say. After we take a knock in this part of the country, we kiss and be friends. But if you had run me through the guts, then I should be dead, and you might go kiss the hangman.

HASTINGS. The rebuke is just. But I must hasten to relieve Miss Neville; if you keep the old lady employed, I promise to take care of the young one.

Exit HASTINGS.

TONY. Never fear me. Here she comes. Vanish. She's got from the pond, and draggled up to the waist like a mermaid.

Enter MRS HARDCASTLE.

MRS HARDCASTLE. Oh, Tony, I'm killed. Shook. Battered to death. I shall never survive it. That last jolt that laid us against the quickset hedge has done my business.

TONY. Alack, mama, it was all your own fault. You would be for running away by night, without knowing one inch of the way.

MRS HARDCASTLE. I wish we were at home again. I never met so many accidents in so short a journey. Drenched in the mud, overturned in a ditch, stuck fast in a slough, jolted to a jelly, and at last to lose our way. Whereabouts do you think we are, Tony?

TONY. By my guess we should be upon Crack-skull Common, about forty miles from home.

MRS HARDCASTLE. O lud! O lud! the most notorious spot in all the country. We only want a robbery to make a complete night on't.

TONY. Don't be afraid, mama, don't be afraid. Two of the five that kept here are hanged, and the other three may not find us. Don't be afraid. Is that a man that's galloping behind us? No; it's only a tree. Don't be afraid.

MRS HARDCASTLE. The fright will certainly kill me.

TONY. Do you see anything like a black hat moving behind the thicket?

MRS HARDCASTLE. O death!

TONY. No, it's only a cow. Don't be afraid, mama; don't be afraid.

MRS HARDCASTLE. As I'm alive, Tony, I see a man coming towards us. Ah! I'm sure on't. If he perceives us we are undone.

TONY (*aside*). Father-in-law, by all that's unlucky, come to take one of his night walks. (*To her.*) Ah, it's a highwayman, with pistols as long as my arm. A damned ill-looking fellow.

MRS HARDCASTLE. Good heaven defend us! He approaches.

TONY. Do you hide yourself in that thicket, and leave me to manage him. If there be any danger I'll cough and cry, Hem! When I cough be sure to keep close.

MRS HARDCASTLE *hides behind a tree in the back scene.*

Enter HARDCASTLE.

HARDCASTLE. I'm mistaken, or I heard voices of people in want of help. Oh, Tony, is that you? I did not expect you so soon back. Are your mother and her charge in safety?

TONY. Very safe, sir, at my aunt Pedigree's. Hem!

MRS HARDCASTLE (*from behind*). Ah death! I find there's danger.

HARDCASTLE. Forty miles in three hours; sure, that's too much, my youngster.

TONY. Stout horses and willing minds make short journeys, as they say. Hem!

MRS HARDCASTLE (*from behind*). Sure he'll do the dear boy no harm.

HARDCASTLE. But I heard a voice here; I should be glad to know from whence it came?

TONY. It was I, sir, talking to myself, sir. I was saying that forty miles in four hours was very good going. Hem! As to be sure it was. Hem! I have got a sort of cold by being out in the air. We'll go in, if you please. Hem!

HARDCASTLE. But if you talked to yourself, you did not answer yourself. I am certain I heard two voices, and am resolved (*Raising his voice.*) to find the other out.

MRS HARDCASTLE (*from behind*). Oh! he's coming to find me out. Oh!

TONY. What need you go, sir, if I tell you. Hem! I'll lay down my life for the truth – hem! – I'll tell you all, sir. (*Detaining him.*)

HARDCASTLE. I tell you, I will not be detained. I insist on seeing. It's in vain to expect I'll believe you.

MRS HARDCASTLE (*running forward from behind*). O lud, he'll murder my poor boy, my darling. Here, good gentleman, whet your rage upon me. Take my money, my life, but spare that young gentleman, spare my child, if you have any mercy.

HARDCASTLE. My wife! as I'm a Christian. From whence can she come, or what does she mean!

MRS HARDCASTLE (*kneeling*). Take compassion on us, good Mr Highwayman. Take our money, our watches, all we have, but spare our lives. We will never bring you to justice, indeed we won't, good Mr Highwayman.

HARDCASTLE. I believe the woman's out of her senses. What, Dorothy, don't you know *me?*

MRS HARDCASTLE. Mr Hardcastle, as I'm alive. My fears blinded me. But who, my dear, could have expected to meet you here, in this frightful place, so far from home? What has brought you to follow us?

HARDCASTLE. Sure, Dorothy, you have not lost your wits? So far from home, when you are within forty yards of your own door? (*To him.*) This is one of your old tricks, you graceless rogue you. (*To her.*) Don't you know the gate, and the mulberry-tree; and don't you remember the horse-pond, my dear?

MRS HARDCASTLE. Yes, I shall remember the horse-pond as long as I live; I have caught my death in it. (*To* TONY.) And it is to you, you graceless varlet, I owe all this? I'll teach you to abuse your mother, I will.

TONY. Ecod, mother, all the parish says you have spoiled me, and so you may take the fruits on't.

MRS HARDCASTLE. I'll spoil you, I will.

Follows him off the stage. Exeunt.

HARDCASTLE. There's morality, however, in his reply.

Exit. Enter HASTINGS *and* MISS NEVILLE.

HASTINGS. My dear Constance, why will you deliberate thus? If we delay a moment, all is lost for ever. Pluck up a little resolution, and we shall soon be out of the reach of her malignity.

MISS NEVILLE. I find it impossible. My spirits are so sunk with the agitations I have suffered, that I am unable to face any new danger. Two or three years' patience will at last crown us with happiness.

HASTINGS. Such a tedious delay is worse than inconstancy. Let us fly, my charmer. Let us date our happiness from this very moment. Perish fortune. Love and content will increase what we possess beyond a monarch's revenue. Let me prevail.

MISS NEVILLE. No, Mr Hastings; no. Prudence once more comes to my relief, and I will obey its dictates. In the moment of passion, fortune may be despised, but it ever produces a lasting repentance. I'm resolved to apply to Mr Hardcastle's compassion and justice for redress.

HASTINGS. But though he had the will, he has not the power to relieve you.

MISS NEVILLE. But he has influence, and upon that I am resolved to rely.

HASTINGS. I have no hopes. But since you persist, I must reluctantly obey you.

Exeunt.

Act V, Scene iii

Scene changes [*to the house*].

Enter SIR CHARLES *and* MISS HARDCASTLE.

SIR CHARLES. What a situation am I in! If what you say appears, I shall then find a guilty son. If what he says be true, I shall then lose one that, of all others, I most wished for a daughter.

MISS HARDCASTLE. I am proud of your approbation, and to show I merit it, if you place yourselves as I directed, you shall hear his explicit declaration. But he comes.

SIR CHARLES. I'll to your father, and keep him to the appointment.

Exit SIR CHARLES. *Enter* MARLOW.

MARLOW. Though prepared for setting out, I come once more to take leave, nor did I, till this moment, know the pain I feel in the separation.

MISS HARDCASTLE (*in her own natural manner*). I believe these sufferings cannot be very great, sir, which you can so easily remove. A day or two longer, perhaps, might lessen your uneasiness, by showing the little value of what you now think proper to regret.

MARLOW (*aside*). This girl every moment improves upon me. (*To her.*) It must not be, madam. I have already trifled too long with my heart. My very pride begins to submit to my passion. The disparity of education and fortune, the anger of a parent, and the contempt of my equals, begin to lose their weight; and nothing can restore me to myself, but this painful effort of resolution.

MISS HARDCASTLE. Then go, sir. I'll urge nothing more to detain you. Though my family be as good as hers you came down to visit, and my education, I hope, not inferior, what are these advantages without equal affluence? I must remain contented with the slight approbation of imputed merit; I must have only the mockery of your addresses, while all your serious aims are fixed on fortune.

Enter HARDCASTLE *and* SIR CHARLES *from behind.*

SIR CHARLES. Here, behind this screen.

HARDCASTLE. Ay, ay, make no noise. I'll engage my Kate covers him with confusion at last.

MARLOW. By heavens, madam, fortune was ever my smallest consideration. Your beauty at first caught my eye; for who could see that without emotion? But every moment that I converse with you, steals in some new grace, heightens the picture, and gives it stronger expression. What at first seemed rustic plainness, now appears refined simplicity. What seemed forward assurance, now strikes me as the result of courageous innocence, and conscious virtue.

SIR CHARLES. What can it mean! He amazes me!

HARDCASTLE. I told you how it would be. Hush!

MARLOW. I am now determined to stay, madam, and I have too good an opinion of my father's discernment, when he sees you, to doubt his approbation.

MISS HARDCASTLE. No, Mr Marlow, I will not, cannot detain you. Do you think I could suffer a connection, in which there is the smallest room for repentance? Do you think I would take the mean advantage of a transient passion, to load you with confusion? Do you think I could ever relish that happiness, which was acquired by lessening yours?

MARLOW. By all that's good, I can have no happiness but what's in your power to grant me. Nor shall I ever feel repentance, but in not having seen your merits before. I will stay, even contrary to your wishes; and though you should persist to shun me, I will make my respectful assiduities atone for the levity of my past conduct.

MISS HARDCASTLE. Sir, I must entreat you'll desist. As our acquaintance began, so let it end, in indifference. I might have given an hour or two to levity; but seriously, Mr Marlow, do you think I could ever submit to a connection, where *I* must appear mercenary, and *you* imprudent? Do you think I could ever catch at the confident addresses of a secure admirer?

MARLOW (*kneeling*). Does this look like security? Does this look like confidence? No, madam, every moment that shows me your merit, only serves to increase my diffidence and confusion. Here let me continue –

SIR CHARLES. I can hold it no longer. Charles, Charles, how hast thou deceived me! Is this your indifference, your uninteresting conversation!

HARDCASTLE. Your cold contempt; your formal interview? What have you to say now?

MARLOW. That I'm all amazement! What can it mean!

HARDCASTLE. It means that you can say and unsay things at pleasure. That you can address a lady in private, and deny it in public; that you have one story for us, and another for my daughter.

MARLOW. Daughter! – this lady your daughter!

HARDCASTLE. Yes, sir, my only daughter. My Kate, whose else should she be?

MARLOW. Oh, the devil.

MISS HARDCASTLE. Yes, sir, that very identical tall squinting lady you were pleased. to take me for. (*Curtseying.*) She that you addressed as the mild, modest, sentimental man of gravity, and the bold forward agreeable Rattle of the Ladies Club; ha! ha! ha!

MARLOW. Zounds, there's no bearing this; it's worse than death.

MISS HARDCASTLE. In which of your characters, sir, will you give us leave to address you? As the faltering gentleman, with looks on the ground, that speaks just to be heard, and hates hypocrisy; or the loud confident creature, that keeps it up with Mrs Mantrap, and old Miss Biddy Buckskin, till three in the morning; ha! ha! ha!

MARLOW. Oh, curse on my noisy head. I never attempted to be impudent yet, that I was not taken down. I must be gone.

HARDCASTLE. By the hand of my body, but you shall not. I see it was all a mistake, and I am rejoiced to find it. You shall not, sir, I tell you. I know she'll forgive you. Won't you forgive him, Kate? We'll all forgive you. Take courage, man.

They retire, she tormenting him, to the back scene.

Enter MRS HARDCASTLE, TONY.

MRS HARDCASTLE. So, so, they're gone off. Let them go, I care not.

HARDCASTLE. Who gone?

MRS HARDCASTLE. My dutiful niece and her gentleman, Mr Hastings, from Town. He who came down with our modest visitor here.

SIR CHARLES. Who, my honest George Hastings? As worthy a fellow as lives, and the girl could not have made a more prudent choice.

HARDCASTLE. Then, by the hand of my body, I'm proud of the connection.

MRS HARDCASTLE. Well, if he has taken away the lady, he has not taken her fortune; that remains in this family to console us for her loss.

HARDCASTLE. Sure Dorothy you would not be so mercenary?

MRS HARDCASTLE. Ay, that's my affair, not yours.

HARDCASTLE. But you know if your son, when of age, refuses to marry his cousin, her whole fortune is then at her own disposal.

MRS HARDCASTLE. Ay, but he's not of age, and she has not thought proper to wait for his refusal.

Enter HASTINGS *and* MISS NEVILLE.

MRS HARDCASTLE (*aside*). What? returned so soon, I begin not to like it.

HASTINGS (*to* HARDCASTLE). For my late attempt to fly off with your niece, let my present confusion be my punishment. We are now come back, to appeal from your justice to your humanity. By her father's consent, I first paid her my addresses, and our passions were first founded in duty.

MISS NEVILLE. Since his death, I have been obliged to stoop to dissimulation to avoid oppression. In an hour of levity, I was ready even to give up my fortune to secure my choice.

But I'm now recovered from the delusion, and hope from your tenderness what is denied me from a nearer connection.

MRS HARDCASTLE. Pshaw, pshaw, this is all but the whining end of a modern novel.

HARDCASTLE. Be it what it will, I'm glad they're come back to reclaim their due. Come hither, Tony boy. Do you refuse this lady's hand whom I now offer you?

TONY. What signifies my refusing? You know I can't refuse her till I'm of age, father.

HARDCASTLE. While I thought concealing your age, boy, was likely to conduce to your improvement, I concurred with your mother's desire to keep it secret. But since I find she turns it to a wrong use, I must now declare, you have been of age these last three months.

TONY. Of age! Am I of age, father?

HARDCASTLE. Above three months.

TONY. Then you'll see the first use I'll make of my liberty. (*Taking* MISS NEVILLE's *hand.*) Witness all men by these presents, that I, Anthony Lumpkin, Esquire, Of BLANK place, refuse you, Constantia Neville, spinster, of no place at all, for my true and lawful wife. So Constance Neville may marry whom she pleases, and Tony Lumpkin is his own man again.

SIR CHARLES. O brave Squire.

HASTINGS. My worthy friend.

MRS HARDCASTLE My undutiful offspring.

MARLOW. Joy, my dear George, I give you joy sincerely. And could I prevail upon my little tyrant here to be less arbitrary, I should be the happiest man alive, if you would return me the favour.

HASTINGS (*to* MISS HARDCASTLE). Come, madam, you are now driven to the very last scene of all your contrivances. I know you like him, I'm sure he loves you, and you must and shall have him.

HARDCASTLE (*joining their hands*). And I say so too. And Mr Marlow, if she makes as good a wife as she has a daughter, I don't believe you'll ever repent your bargain. So now to supper, tomorrow we shall gather all the poor of the parish about us, and the Mistakes of the Night shall be crowned with a merry morning; so, boy, take her; and as you have been mistaken in the mistress, my wish is, that you may never be mistaken in the wife.

Epilogue

by Dr Goldsmith

Well, having stooped to conquer with success,
And gained a husband without aid from dress,
Still as a Barmaid, I could wish it too,
As I have conquered him to conquer you:
And let me say, for all your resolution,
That pretty Barmaids have done execution.
Our life is all a play, composed to please,
We have our exits and our entrances.
The first act shows the simple country maid,
Harmless and young, of every thing afraid;
Blushes when hired, and with unmeaning action,
'I hopes as how to give you satisfaction.'
Her second act displays a livelier scene. –
Th'unblushing Barmaid of a country inn.
Who whisks about the house, at market caters,
Talks loud, coquets the guests, and scolds the waiters.
Next the scene shifts to town, and there she soars,
The chop house toast of ogling connoisseurs.
On Squires and Cits she there displays her arts,
And on the gridiron broils her lovers' hearts
And as she smiles, her triumphs to complete,
Even Common Councilmen forget to eat.
The fourth act shows her wedded to the Squire,
And Madam now begins to hold it higher;
Pretends to taste, at Operas cries, *Caro*,
And quits her Nancy Dawson, for *Che faro*.

Dotes upon dancing, and in all her pride,
Swims round the room, the *Heinel* of Cheapside:
Ogles and leers with artificial skill,
Till having lost in age the power to kill,
She sits all night at cards, and ogles at spadille.
Such, through our lives, the eventful history
The fifth and last act still remains for me.
The Barmaid now for your protection prays,
Turns Female Barrister, and pleads for Bayes.

Glossary

Allons – (French) Let's go

Ally Croaker – an Irish popular song

Ariadne – opera by Handel

basket – the luggage compartment of a stage-coach, also used by poor passengers

baskets – hand guards on swords

bobs – ear rings

brazen-nosed – brass-tipped (against heat)

Brooks, George – a fictional character invented by Goldsmith, part of Hardcastle's fantasies about the War of the Spanish Succession

Bully Dawson – a well-known bully

Bayes – name given to dramatists (after the character in Buckingham's *The Rehearsal*); also the laurel wreath given to a poet, hence applause

Caro – (Italian) superb

Che faro – An aria from Gluck's opera *Orfeo*

Cherry . . . Stratagem – the Landlord's daughter in Farquhar's play; see introduction

circumbendibus – roundabout route to complete the circle

Colman – George Colman the Elder, dramatist and manager of Covent Garden Theatre

Complete Huswif – a popular household handbook

consumptive – suffering from tuberculosis

Corporation of Bedford – like guilds, corporations were notorious for their gluttony

Crooked Lane – Cannon Street; not an obvious fashion centre

Darby and Joan – proverbial happily-married old couple

degagée – (French) stylish

Denain – a town besieged in 1712 by troops under Prince
    Eugene, not Marlborough

duchesses of Drury Lane – prostitutes

Dullissimo Macaroni – most stupid fop

elevens – the eleven (excluding Judas) apostles?

Eugene, Prince – one of the allied generals in the War of the
    Spanish Succession

father-in-law – step-father

Friseur – (French) hairdresser

Garrick, David – leading actor and theatre manager of the period

Gothic – barbarous

haspicholls – Tony's version of harpsichord

head – in II, refers to Mrs Hardcastle's hairstyle

Heinel – Anna-Frederica Heinel, a leading professional dancer

Hyder Ali . . . Ali Khan – Indian rulers of the period in conflict
    with the British

improvements – (landscaped) gardens

incontinently – immediately

inoculation – inoculation against smallpox, introduced in 1718,
    was widespread by 1773

izzard – the letter Z

Johnson, Samuel – leading literary figure, famous for compiling a
    major English Dictionary

Joiners Company – a City of London guild famous for its banquets

jorum – a punchbowl

Ladies Club – an actual club where Goldsmith himself had made
    a reputation

Lethes . . . Styxes . . . Stygians – in classical mythology Lethe and
    Styx are rivers; Stygian is the adjective from Styx

Lion . . . Angel . . . Lamb – typical names for inn rooms

longitude – a reliable method of calculating longitude was one of
    the key intellectual and technological challenges of the

century; a long standing reward for solving the problem was claimed some three months after the play was first produced

Marlborough, Duke of – one of the allied generals in the War of the Spanish Succession

mauvaise honte – awkwardness

morris – get moving

murrain – disease

Nancy Dawson – a famous hornpipe dancer and/or the song named after her

nicked seven . . . ames ace – made a winning throw at dice (seven) without then throwing two ones

Pantheon . . . Grotto Gardens . . . Borough – a fashionable tea house, a down-market pleasure garden and the London Borough of Southwark, no longer by 1773 a fashionable residential area (Mrs Hardcastle is showing her ignorance)

paste . . . marcasites – costume jewellery (the ladies pawn their jewels and bring back fakes but Mrs Hardcastle appears not to understand what's going on)

pigeon – as well as the bird, a fool or dupe

Quincy – John Quincy's *Complete English Dispensatory*, a popular book of remedies

Quis . . . Quaes . . . Quods – Tony's versions of Latin pronouns

Rake's Progress – Hogarth's popular series of engravings

Ranelagh . . . St James's . . . Tower Wharf – a public pleasure garden; a fashionable area and an unfashionable area (linked by Hastings to show up Mrs Hardcastle)

receipt – prescription

rumbling – an obsolescent form of 'rambling'; ironic given the speaker's love of novelty

Scandalous Magazine – see tête-à-tête

shake-bag – fighting cock

shaking pudding – jelly

Shuter – Ned Shuter, a comic actor, who was the original Hardcastle *spadille* – the ace of spades in the card game ombre

tablets – note book

tête – hair-piece

tête-à-tête – (French) private conversation between two people; in II, specifically the illustrations published in the *Town and Country Magazine* of prominent men and their mistress

tiff-taff-taffety cream – probably a form of blancmange

us that sell ale – Hardcastle means something like 'those of us who work' but Marlow and Hastings take him literally

'Water Parted' – from Thomas Arne's opera *Artaxerxes*

Westminster Hall – the law courts

Whistlejacket – a famous race horse

Woodward – Henry Woodward, a comic actor who turned down the part of Tony Lumpkin in the original production

woundily – extremely